Stories of Encounter

Pray Now Prayers, Devotions, Blessings
and Reflections on 'How They Prayed'

Published on behalf of
THE CHURCH OF SCOTLAND
MISSION AND DISCIPLESHIP COUNCIL

SAINT ANDREW PRESS
Edinburgh

First published in 2017 by Saint Andrew Press
SAINT ANDREW PRESS
121 George Street
Edinburgh EH2 4YN

Copyright © Resourcing Worship Team, Mission and Discipleship
Council, the Church of Scotland 2017

ISBN 978 0 71520 987 5

Please note that the views expressed in *Pray Now* are those of the
individual writer and not necessarily the official view of
the Church of Scotland, which can be laid down only by the
General Assembly.

British Library Cataloguing in Publication Data
A catalogue record for this book is available from the
British Library.

It is the publisher's policy to use only papers that are natural and
recyclable and that have been manufactured from timber grown in
renewable, properly managed forests. All of the manufacturing
processes of the papers are expected to conform to the
environmental regulations of the country of origin.

Typeset by Hugh Hillyard-Parker, Edinburgh
Printed and bound in the United Kingdom by CPI Group (UK) Ltd

Contents

Preface   vi

Using this Book   vii

Encounters with Yourself

  1   Fragility   2
  2   Mystery   4
  3   Fear   8
  4   Control / Loss of Control   10
  5   Not Yourself   12
  6   Body Image   14
  7   Sexuality   16
  8   Emptiness   18
  9   Reflection   20
 10   Shadow   22
 11   Contentment   24
 12   Success   26
 13   Hope   28

Encounters with People

 14   Siblings   32
 15   Parents   34
 16   Neighbours   36
 17   Friends   38
 18   Authorities   40
 19   Them   42
 20   Politicians   44
 21   Enemies   46
 22   Strangers   48
 23   Refugees   50
 24   Those Who Serve Us   52
 25   Cold Callers   54
 26   Church Folk   56

Encounters with the World

27	Thresholds	60
28	Weather	62
29	Animals	64
30	Mountains	66
31	Valleys	68
32	Desert	70
33	Water	72
34	Moor	74
35	Trees	76
36	Cave	78
37	City	80
38	Traffic Jam	82
39	Phone Box	84

Encounters with Jesus

40	Would-be Disciple	88
41	A Positive Reaction to Jesus' Teaching	90
42	A Negative Reaction to Jesus' Teaching	92
43	Disabled	94
44	Young People	96
45	Old People	98
46	Women	100
47	Foreigner	102
48	Roman	104
49	Moneylenders	106
50	General Crowd	108
51	Friends	110
52	Disciples	112

How They Prayed

1	St Benedict of Nursia	118
2	St Columba	122
3	St Hildegard of Bingen	126
4	St Francis of Assisi	130
5	Julian of Norwich	134
6	St Ignatius of Loyola	138
7	John Knox	142
8	St Teresa of Ávila	146
9	James Melville	150
10	John Wesley	154
11	Thomas Merton	158
12	Mother Teresa	162

Acknowledgements	166

Preface

Encounters shape us. They leave their marks of blessing or wounding on our lives. This book helps us to bring our stories of encounter to God.

The Bible is rich in stories of encounter; it speaks of a God who meets with people. The way in which John's Gospel introduces Jesus bristles with the expectation of encounter:

> *The Word became flesh and blood,*
> *and moved into the neighbourhood.*
> *We saw the glory with our own eyes.*
>
> ~ John 1:14 ('The Message') ~

The writers of the 52 meditations and prayers in this book lead us into God's presence. Their words encourage us to come to God with our own stories of encounter – with ourselves, with other people, with the world around us, and with Jesus.

Christians are part of a procession; others have gone before us, and others will come after us. When we find it hard to express our stories of encounter in prayer, there is a rich heritage of experience to inspire us. A feature of this book is the 'How They Prayed' section: a set of articles based on twelve historical figures widely regarded as having contributed to the prayer life of the Church. Their example will inspire and encourage us.

Our stories of encounter may be filled with many different emotions. The writers of this book help us find words to speak about these stories with God. It's a book to keep using – we'll find God's grace and peace as we turn its pages.

REVD DAN CARMICHAEL
Convenor, Resourcing Worship

Using this Book

*Then Jacob woke from his sleep and said, 'Surely the
Lord is in this place – and I did not know it!' And he
was afraid, and said, 'How awesome is this place!
This is none other than the house of God, and this is
the gate of heaven.'*

~ Genesis 28:16-17 ~

God meets with people – that's a theme that the Bible
records from the earliest times. As Jacob found,
encounters with God can be hard to recognise at first.
This book leads us to reflect on the stories of encounter
that have filled our lives so far and that draw us to God.

'Stories of Encounter' is the theme of this edition of
Pray Now. Although the title links the book to the
Church of Scotland's theme for 2018, this is a book for
people of all church backgrounds and none.

The book is in two sections – the first contains
meditations and prayers, while the second contains a
series of articles on 'How They Prayed', exploring the
lives of twelve historical figures widely regarded as
having contributed to the prayer life of the Church.

In the first section there are 52 chapters arranged under
four headings that reflect different stories of encounter:

- Encounters with Yourself
- Encounters with People
- Encounters with the World
- Encounters with Jesus

The chapters are written by a broad range of writers, but the structure of each chapter is the same:

- Scripture verse that links to the chapter heading
- Meditation
- Morning Prayer
- Evening Prayer
- Two suggested Scripture readings
- Blessing

Use the book in the way that is most helpful to you. The 52 chapters mean that a different chapter can be focused on during each week of the year, offering a stimulus for worship or devotion over a seven-day span. However, the chapters can also be used in any order. Some of them reflect particular circumstances of life and could be used at specific times. The chapters can be used for individual prayer, for praying in a family, for praying with a friend, for praying in small groups, and for praying in a service of worship.

The words of each chapter have been written with great care, but there can be times when the words of others don't seem to speak to the situation of the moment. The prayers and meditations included here are not an end in themselves, but a springboard for prayer. Sometimes, the heading or a particular phrase will be enough to lead the reader into their own prayers, whether silent or spoken. A few blank pages have been left so that you can note down your own prayers or record ways prayers have been answered in the story of your own life.

The second section of the book contains twelve articles on 'How They Prayed'. Each of the twelve writers has contributed a reflection drawing on the rich example of prayer from a notable historical figure of the past. At the end of each article is a page that is left blank for notes.

As these articles are read, each reader will bring their own experience and insights; these can be written down and perhaps shared with others.

It is the hope of all those involved in preparing the words of this book that God will use them to help people pray in the midst of life now.

REVD DAN CARMICHAEL

For more information, the guide *How to Pray* can be found on the Church of Scotland website at www.churchofscotland. org.uk/worship or phone 0131 225 5722 and ask to be put through to the Mission and Discipleship Council.

ENCOUNTERS WITH YOURSELF

*For now we see in a mirror, dimly, but then
we will see face to face. Now I know only
in part; then I will know fully, even as I have
been fully known.*

~ 1 Corinthians 13:12 ~

Fragility

He remembers that we are dust.

~ Psalm 103:14 ~

Meditation

Is not faith born of hope
rather than certainty?

Is not resurrection an experience
rather than the position of an empty tomb?

Is not God a relationship with love
rather than a being in the sky?

Is not church a risk
rather than a listed building?

Is not an angel an exclamation of 'alleluia'
rather than a being with wings?

Is not all we believe taken on trust
rather than confirmed with proof?

Is not such faith a fragile relationship,
for is it not the risk God takes in loving us
and anticipating us loving God back?

Morning Prayer

May this day
be gentle with what is fragile:
the questions I shape
and the dreams I have;
may this day
kindly nurture
the beginnings I make
and the endings I face;
and may this day,
with all that is vulnerable
in me and my world,
be held completely
by You.

Evening Prayer

In the meeting places of today
and the encounters with others,
in the pain and hurts of letting go
and the cries of birthing new life,
may I place Your word of blessing
on all that has gifted me today
an insight into how precious,
valuable,
subtle,
Your grace has been;
and though gentle and fragile grace might appear,
may I give thanks
for how it has enriched and loved my fragile world
today.   AMEN

Scripture Readings

Psalm 103:6–18   *Steadfast love*
Matthew 6:25–34   *Lilies of the field*

Blessing

May your questions be blessed,
your longings honoured,
your vulnerability nurtured,
by the God whose love
is as fragile and unmistakable
as the footprints of the gardener
in the grass that first dawn.   AMEN

Mystery

*In the morning, while it was still very dark, He got up
and went out to a deserted place, and there He prayed.*

~ Mark 1:35 ~

Meditation

'Lech lecha',
'Go to yourself',
God told Abram:
discover in the soul's fathomless depths
the *Shekinah** huddled within;
secret, hidden, luminous.
In the soul's solitude
illimitable darkness, impenetrable;
in the Holy of Holies
sheerest silence,
serene.

Alone?
In the sphere of dreams,
an inner world of myth, metaphor
and wondering,
abandoning images,
self-images, god-images,
that constrict and confine,
wrestling with demons and devils,
encountering Mystery, Nothingness,
entering the truer self.

Like Mary at the feet of Jesus gazing,
like Thomas feeling the warmth of Christ's wounds,
like Paul caught away in the Third Heaven,
in stillness I open myself
to Christ, cosmic consciousness,
spiritual evolution,
at one with the Sacred in all things.

**in Hebrew, the dwelling-place of God
or the divine presence of God*

How can it be that alone
I, enfleshed, encounter the Eternal?
In the womb of my soul
the baby of Bethlehem,
is alive in me.
I am never so complete,
so absorbed in the Absolute,
as when I am alone,
embraced, tenderly held.
Sublime, ineffable:
ecstasy.
Dark, deserted:
the paradox of Presence.

Morning Prayer

I wake to myself,
to my life,
to the blessings and the burdens,
the cares and the concerns,
to my regular prayers,
to another day's routine,
to words and more words.

I wake again to my truer Self,
to the Tender Transcendence within me,
to the Spirit holding in being
every cell and soul,
every consciousness that has ever been;
I wake to the Elusive,
whose eloquent silence
echoes in every human heart,
in all that is.

Sustain me with the Emptiness
that fills all things.   AMEN

Evening Prayer

Turning aside,
like Moses at the burning bush,
more listening than talking,
enveloped by vastness,
a call to leave *Mitzrayim**,
a tight place, a constricted place,
to journey to a new land:
wider possibilities.

Let me look back over today
to see You again, as if for the first time.
I am richly blessed.
Help me to keep moving forward,
pondering intuitions pregnant with meaning,
answering Your muffled call,
to move ever more deeply into You.   AMEN

Scripture Readings

Mark 1:32–39   *Amidst the demands, Jesus prays*
Colossians 1:15–20   *Christ of the cosmos*

Blessing

Crucify within me
all that diminishes
my humanity;
raise up within me
the Immortal,
the divine image,
my truer self,
God-bearer.   AMEN

* *the Hebrew word for Egypt meaning 'a tight place,
a place of constriction'*

PRAYER NOTES

Fear

'Fear gripped me, and my bones trembled.'

~ Job 4:14 (NLT) ~

Meditation

Fears assault us.
Whether within us or around us,
whether simple anxieties about social skills,
about being liked, or about performance.
Fears penetrate;
hold us hostage in a house of fear.
What are the fears that terrorise you?
When do they come to you?
How do they grip you?
This is *pachad,*[†]
the fear, the dread, the terror
that exposes us and makes our lives feel vulnerable;
that diminishes and cripples us at times.

Yet… ponder this –
God is our shelter, the secret place.
You are invited to consider *samekh*[‡]
meaning to lean upon, to uphold or to support.

Meditate on the shape,
a small vessel with a lid or roof over it.
A shelter.
Let it be a vessel to place your fears;
a simple reminder of God's sheltering, upholding,
supporting.

[†] *the Hebrew word for fear, dread, terror – projected
  or imagined*
[‡] *the 15th letter of the Hebrew alphabet*

Morning Prayer

Whatever the fears that arise today,
I will not be bound nor overwhelmed.
I will lean upon You Lord.
I will trust in You,
confident that You uphold and support me.   Amen

Evening Prayer

As I shape my hand like the *samekh*
I fill it with the fears that came over me today.
I place each one in this vessel,
under the sheltering cover of Your loving presence.
Content, I leave them there and am in their grip no more.
Your perfect love is stronger than fear and drives it out.
This night I place myself in the *samekh*,
the sheltering of Your care.
There Lord,
restore my soul this night.

> *Alone with none but thee, my God,*
> *I journey on my way.*
> *What need I fear, when thou art near*
> *O king of night and day?*
> *More safe am I within thy hand*
> *Than if a host did round me stand.*   Amen
>
> *~ Adapted from prayer of St Columba ~*

Scripture Readings

Job 4.12–14	*Eliphaz's experience of fear*
Psalm 91	*Under His wings*

Blessing

The sheltering wings of the Father be your refuge.
The encompassing love of the Son be your strength.
The upholding of the Holy Spirit, be your peace.
Each night and each day, each day and each night.
Amen

Control / Loss of Control

Why have You forsaken me?

~ Psalm 22:1 ~

Meditation

Life will often teach
that to be in control
is to hide your emotions.

But I rejoice in God,
Who lets me be myself,
Who invites my honest thoughts
and only desires my open heart.

Life will often teach
that the expected response
is to say 'I'm fine'.

But I rejoice in God,
Who hears my cries,
Who invites my doubts and questions
and is always faithful.

This day,
I will be honest before God,
and in God, I will find my rest.

Morning Prayer

I trust in You, Holy One,
for I am created and known by You.
You have made me as I am,
and know my deepest thoughts and needs.

Help me find in You this day,
the peace that passes all understanding.

In the empty spaces, and in the searching places,
let me trust in Your love
and find my hope renewed.
Gentle Spirit, be my companion.

Powerful Spirit, be my strength.
Transforming Spirit, be my inspiration.   Amen

Evening Prayer

Gracious God,
in the day and night,
I doubt myself at times,
and doubt in You.

But You always draw me back,
not in order to control me,
but to release me.
You are the God who sets Your people free,
to live in fullness and to thrive.
May Your Spirit live in me.

I pray this night for all who are struggling,
with themselves or with others,
with circumstances beyond their control.
You are ever faithful,
always near,
and You invite us to let go,
and find Your peace.

Let it be found in me.   Amen

Scripture Readings

> Psalm 22:1–11   *Honest before God*
> John 14:25–27   *Finding peace*

Blessing

> In the love of God,
> in the life of Christ,
> in the peace of the Spirit,
> I am found.   Amen

Not Yourself

God said to Moses, 'I AM WHO I AM.'

~ Exodus 3:14 ~

Meditation

Here I am;
the great I AM NOT.
NOT ready to lead.
NOT equipped to judge.
NOT prepared for a wayward world.
NOT brave enough for wilderness wandering.
NOT for a long time.

WHO AM I
to be chosen
to speak with wisdom,
to carry the weight of others,
to see the signs,
to seek the pathway,
to make the sacrifice?

I run from danger when it strikes,
nurse my pain like a disease,
thirst for life in my veins
and hesitate to ask for my brother's help.

Yet here I am, Lord,
all set for adventures in your kingdom.
For only with You
am I myself.

Morning Prayer

Each day, Lord,
is the opportunity to be someone else.
Someone kinder and gentler,
someone wiser and braver,
someone calmer and quieter.

But I am who I am
and I will be who I will be this day.
Remind me,
as I seek to leave a little of my selfish self behind,
that I am loved and cherished for being me.
Help me,
to accept others as themselves,
remembering they too are Yours.
Most of all, Lord, be Yourself.   AMEN

Evening Prayer

Whatever I have seen this day
whatever I have been this day,
I have tried to be faithful
to You and to myself, Lord.
But You know better than anyone
those moments when my mouth said one thing
and my heart another.
So now I hand myself over
to be rested and renewed in You
that tomorrow I may be who
You want me to be.   AMEN

Scripture Readings

Exodus 3:7—4:20   *God calls Moses*
2 Corinthians 5:17   *A new creation in Christ*

Blessing

Take, oh take me as I am;
Summon out what I shall be;
Set Your seal upon my heart
And live in me.   AMEN

~ John L. Bell ~

Body Image

*Let your adornment be the inner self with the lasting
beauty of a gentle and quiet spirit, which is very
precious in God's sight.*

~ 1 Peter 3:4 ~

Meditation

I cannot see the scar on my back,
but I can feel the tightness
of skin pulled together after surgery,
new nerve endings regenerating,
itching me to scratch and complain.
The rivets of surgical scarring
sear across my back – a reminder of what happened.

And now, it's back.
Cancerous cells, regenerating and multiplying,
threatening to carve out my body,
snuffing hope.
The glinting scalpel
will slice out wide margins –
or at least that's what the doctors hope for.
My body might never be the same;
I might never have that beach figure
I was once in touching distance of.

Seven, deep scars might invite body shaming.
But, for me,
they represent a life yet to be lived,
the very assurance of things hoped for,
and the conviction of that which is unseen.
God willing.

Morning Prayer

Lord God,
give me the courage to face this new day,
appreciating what is really important.
Help me not to be seduced by the image of life,
but to appreciate true, inner beauty,
given by You.   AMEN

Evening Prayer

Loving God, we pray for all concerned with cancer.

For scientists and researchers, pursuing cures.

For surgeons and doctors and nurses, and carers.

For those who have just received diagnosis,
and for those who are in the throes of fighting
with every fibre of their being.

For those who will win,
and for those who will lose,
and for the ones who will hold their hands,
this night and every night.   AMEN

Scripture Readings

1 Peter 3:3–4   *Inner beauty*
Ephesians 2:8–10   *We are God's handiwork*

Blessing

Above all things, know this:
you are loved
graciously, reverently and wholly;
no matter who you are,
God loves you.   AMEN

Sexuality

My frame was not hidden from You,
when I was being made in secret,
intricately woven in the depths of the earth.

~ Psalm 139:15 ~

Meditation

In all this intricate,
intimate glory,
here I am, framed,
forming crystal-like
– naked –
as man–woman
in this womb,
before the one who
created all.

Who I am,
will emerge for the world
to know and see in due course.

How I am
received
in all my bodily,
sexual, uniqueness
is out of my
power. I take
courage from the
bold embodiment
of the one who goes before.

For now, here I am,
– en-wombed –
orientated
around a
Love that frees,
and delights
in the whole of me.

Morning Prayer

Loving Christ who came to us
embodied, go with me this day.
Surround me, and all You love with
courage to be fully ourselves;
faith to know that we are loved;
cheerfulness to walk lightly on the earth;
and joy in the delight of our bodies. AMEN

Evening Prayer

Dear Lord, as I re-orientate myself
around You this evening,
I give thanks for the day.

I hold before You tenderly
those persecuted for who they are.

I hold before You tenderly
those afraid of the secrets their body holds.

I hold before You tenderly
our faith community as we navigate a way towards
a world that is loving, inclusive and true.
In Jesus' name. AMEN

Scripture Readings

Psalm 139:13–16	*You knit me together in my mother's womb*
1 Corinthians 11:24	*'This is my body'*

Blessing

May the blessing of the Divine Lover,
who delights in us,
body, mind and spirit,
be with us now and always. AMEN

Emptiness

My God, my God, why have You forsaken me?

~ Psalm 22:1 ~

Meditation

Darkness.
Silence.
Both enveloping this moment,
removing views of new horizons.
I am broken.
Dreams and plans for tomorrows
no longer possible.
No hope,
crushing imagination,
lost ambition.

All time stands still,
as the long dark night of the soul
plunges deeper into the endless well of nothing.
Not even tears
to restore an awareness of being.
Will morning come?

Morning Prayer

Why have You forsaken me Lord?
I am trying to hold,
to hang onto my faith
that even in this barren land You are there.
But the thought of today faced alone again
weighs heavy in my heart.
Please don't forsake me,
but meet me in the darkness.   AMEN

Evening Prayer

In the shadows cast by fading light
I am searching for the spark or flicker
that will ignite a passion for another day.
Exhausted by nothing,
I have not found the crumbs of hope
to feast upon and be restored.
Presence of heaven,
come to the doorway of my empty tomb,
and call me back to life.   AMEN

Scripture Readings

Psalm 22	*Plea for release from suffering*
Matthew 27:45–53	*Christ broken on the cross*

Blessing

Encircle me with the blessing
of Your hope for me,
Holy One and Parent,
that I may be released from this womb
into the light of Your love.   AMEN

Reflection

I will know fully, even as I have been fully known.

~ 1 Corinthians 13:12 ~

Meditation

Who is this looking back?
Eyes deep with seeing,
brows furrowed with thinking,
complexion kissed by the wind,
lips anticipating a smile,
dimples deepening,
laughter lines, living proof,
ears restraining strands
escaped from the high-held bun.

Who is this looking back?
We will never see our faces,
but for the tip of the nose.
Held only in the gaze of another,
known least by ourselves,
only ever a reflection in the mirror,
darkened glass or the stillness of water.
The face of a friend or of a stranger?
The face of kindness or harsh with fear?

A dim reflection is a relative thing.
Isn't the bright shining of the moon
but a dim reflection
of the brilliance of the sun?
And what does this face looking back reflect?
On what beauty and tragedy,
what glory and grit
have these eyes gazed?
Who is this looking back?

Morning Prayer

God, who knows us fully,
we turn our face towards You,
where all pretence is exposed,
all hiding denied and
all of life laid bare.
And before we update any status
or present a different face to the world,
we look to You, Your word and world,
to remind and mould us
into who and whose we are.
May we reflect, even if dimly,
the wonder that it is
to be fully known.   AMEN

Evening Prayer

As we take a moment to reflect
on the day that has passed;
on all whom we have encountered
and who have encountered us;
on all that has brought us joy
and gladness, pain or hurt;
on all that we have thought, said and done;
we give thanks in these moments of reflection
and we pray that in some way, even if dimly,
we may have reflected You
as the moon reflects the sun.   AMEN

Scripture Readings

1 Corinthians 13:7–13   *Now we see only a dim reflection*
Numbers 6:22–27   *May His face shine upon you*

Blessing

May the Lord bless you and keep you.
May the Lord make His face to shine upon you,
and may His grace and peace fill you
and be reflected to all you encounter.   AMEN

Shadow

I will give you the treasures of darkness
and riches hidden in secret places,
so that you may know that it is I, the Lord,
the God of Israel, who call you by your name.

~ Isaiah 45:3 ~

Meditation

Aged three I walked up the street with my Gran.
'I have a little shadow that goes in and out with me'
she said, as Robert Louis Stevenson said before.
And so I met my shadow for the first time.
An outer expression of a dark
and sometimes distorted part inside me.

Giver of life, may I embrace the shadow within me,
willing to look, to wonder, to honour that which
often has no clear shape or form:
a wandering, elusive 'something'
that will not quite reveal itself fully.

Often my shadow is dark when I look,
confusing, hard to be with,
yet pointing to some truth I am not quite ready to hear,
calling me into awareness,
asking me to pay attention.

And just sometimes my shadow overwhelms me,
and I feel that I have no substance,
that I am not fully myself;
I have no ground beneath my feet;
I have lost the colour in my life;
all is flat and one-dimensional.

You made me,
and You do not abandon me.
You sit with me in my shadows.
Together may we breathe life into that dark place ...
... until the light comes.

Morning Prayer

In this day – may I accept whatever mixture
of light and dark comes my way,
learning to pay heed to the shadowy moments,
to what they are telling me,
– something not yet quite clear,
an edge of awareness
not yet bathed in light.
Grace me with the wisdom to take note, and to watch,
as the watchman waits for the dawn ...   AMEN

Evening Prayer

Loving and wise God,
in my shadowy and dark moments,
come to me,
make me to know Your presence,
to listen and hear Your love in such inner experience
and reveal to me what I need.

Enable me to be alongside others
in their times of shade,
not trying to fix or sort or make them better,
accepting them as they are,
trusting in Your grace for them,
willing to sit with them and their shadow.   AMEN

Scripture Readings

Psalm 130   *Out of the depths*
Isaiah 45:1–19   *Finding God in the dark*

Blessing

God of the dark and the light,
enter with me into the daily darkness
in a way that helps me know more clearly
that darkness gives birth to light.
As a child in the womb comes into the light,
may I come into each day in expectation
of new things to live and learn.   AMEN

Contentment

And the peace of God, which surpasses all
understanding, will guard your hearts ...

~ Philippians 4:7 ~

Meditation

A contentment based on what you *are* is a
powerful thing.
A contentment based on what you *have* is a
precarious thing.
What you have can be taken, broken, destroyed.
What you are
– the fact that you are made in the image of God –
never can be.

I am created by God.
God is. God is good. God is good enough.
I learn,
I am content. I am whole. I am enough.

This contentment is inalienable, irrevocable,
and priceless.
I can reject it, discount it or take it for granted,
but it's not going anywhere.

This contentment is a powerful quality in a society
predicated on
our appetite, restlessness, and unease.
We are often cast as discontent, incontinent,
malcontents
always needing more.
It is powerful to say, 'No, I'm content.'

This feeling of content is not an excuse to be complacent;
we are called to life in all its fullness
and so should have a hunger for the kingdom,
for justice, for restoration,
but we don't act from uneasy dissatisfaction or greed.
We are not rebels without a cause.

We are content.
In our meal – the Lord's Supper –
there is enough for everyone.
We don't need to be rebels to prove ourselves worthy.

Morning Prayer

Dear God,
help us to be content in ourselves,
content in You,
content in our relationships,
and content to act.   AMEN

Evening Prayer

Dear God,
as the day closes, we loosen
the tight grasp,
the firm grip,
the white knuckles.
We place our hand in Your much larger hand
and breathe deeper.   AMEN

Scripture Readings

Philippians 4:4–20   *Rejoice in the Lord always*
Jeremiah 29:4–9   *Seek the welfare of the city*

Blessing

Surprise us with contentment,
when we are unsuspecting,
in the midst of fretting or grumbling.
At other times
when we feel uneasy and claustrophobic,
gritty and uncomfortable
– looking inward –
gift us with a new restlessness,
a spirit of curiosity and wonder.   AMEN

Success

'Only be strong and very courageous, being careful to act in accordance with all the law that my servant Moses commanded you; do not turn from it to the right hand or to the left, so that you may be successful wherever you go.'

~ Joshua 1:7 ~

Meditation

I walked the line, kept my balance.
I saw the challenge through with requisite discipline,
and now I encounter my reward!
The achievement, the pride!
This moment tastes sweet.

But it's a heady brew, success.
I sample a little, then a little more.
The thirst for this taste grows,
each gulp not unpleasant.
Woozy with it, I'm dull to God.
Lost my bearings, lost my balance.
There's a hangover coming.

But measured, it's a pleasant blessing,
a delicacy gifted by the God who makes me able.
Something to share, something to enjoy,
something to give thanks for;
another way to give glory
to the only One who never fails.

Morning Prayer

Lord, You know what lies before me today,
the hurdles where I may smile as I clear them
or fall as I clatter into them.

Grant me success, O Lord.
Let me approach each challenge
with Your law as the 'how' I do it
and Your glory as the 'why' I do it.

Grant me success, O Lord.
If it should not come, let me be content in You.
It it should come, let me know how to handle it.
Come what may – let me be singing
when the evening comes.   AMEN

Evening Prayer

Lord, thank You for the success I have tasted;
for the things I look back over with satisfaction;
for the gifts and abilities You gave me
to undertake what I did;
for the strength and opportunities You gave me
to see it through.

Thank You for the experience of success,
how it lifts me, boosts me,
puts new vigour in my living.

But at the close of the day, this I will say:
I give all the glory to You,
the Lord who gave me all this.   AMEN

Scripture Readings

Joshua 1:6–9   *Obeying God brings success*
Philippians 3:3–9   *Knowing Christ surpasses success*

Blessing

May God bless you and enlarge your border.
May God's hand be with you.
May God keep you from hurt and harm.   AMEN

~ Adapted from 1 Chronicles 4:10 ~

Hope

Jesus ... said of him, 'Here is truly an Israelite in whom there is no deceit!'

~ John 1:47 ~

Meditation

Didn't You know my reputation?
Didn't You know what they called me
and how proud I was to wear the badge:
sceptic.
Disdainful by default.

I knew Your reputation.
I knew what they called You:
Nazarene.
But to add Messiah?
Impossible.

But caring little for likelihoods,
and less for labels,
You came.
You knew me before I knew myself.
You saw me
and let me unbury the hidden treasure of hope
in a field of longing.
Nazarene Messiah?
You gave me back
a passion for the possible.

Morning Prayer

Jesus, there were days
when You wept, raged, simmered with frustration
and got weary to the bone.
But You did not despair.
'How long?' You cried.
'How little faith!'
'Woe to you!'
'What is lawful?'
But never, *'I give up.'*

You drove out traders,
lambasted the self-righteous,
confronted squabbling friends,
called out hypocrisy,
but never threw in the towel.
'Why do you call me "Lord, Lord", ' You asked,
'and do not do what I tell you?'
'Why are you trying to trap me?'
'Why do you ask for a sign?'
'Why do you not believe me?'
But never, *'Why do I bother?'*

As we walk together into this day, Jesus,
breathe hope into every cell of me!
Let me keep that dogged pilot light,
that is Your Spirit,
alive and well.   AMEN

Evening Prayer

Faith, hope, love …
Lord, if the greatest is love,
how do You rank the other two?
What staying power does hope have in me?
Will hope abide here?
Is hope among my trinity of lasting qualities?
Made in Your image, I affirm the confidence
rooted more firmly than all that can be torn apart.
I stand in solidarity with all who need reacquainted
with that inner trust
in self and in You, the Maker of every self.   AMEN

Scripture Readings

John 1:43–51   *Jesus affirms a sceptic*
Sirach 34:14–20   *No need to be timid*

Blessing

May God bring sparkle to our eyes,
tingles to our imagining.
firmness to our footsteps,
lightness to our carrying.   AMEN

ENCOUNTERS
WITH PEOPLE

*'I give you a new commandment, that you
love one another. Just as I have loved you,
you also should love one another. By this
everyone will know that you are my disciples,
if you have love for one another.'*

~ John 13:34–35 ~

Siblings

'Am I my brother's keeper?'

~ Genesis 4:9 ~

Meditation

Right there in the beginning
is a story of two brothers;
and the earth still cries out
with the blood of Abel.

But they are hardly the only ones:
Isaac and Ishmael,
Jacob and Esau,
Joseph and his brothers.

The Bible will only disappoint
if you seek a perfect, model family,
yet in these complex sibling rivalries
God has decided to set free
the impulse of love.

Then, it was between just a few.
Now there are many more siblings:
denominations,
faiths,
nations,
but the love, always bigger than one side,
is still the same.

Morning Prayer

In the possibilities unfolding in this day
may I be encouraged with moments
to speak words
that shape a love
that shares a space
with my brothers and sisters
whose names I do not know,

and reveal there
through grace and welcome
a love
greater than any side
and bigger than us all.   AMEN

Evening Prayer

From this day, O God,
I offer You my rivalries,
my hurts,
my arguments that took sides
on affairs that didn't matter,
and let You redeem them tonight,
so that on the morrow
I might find new ways to grow
with my brother and sister
into the humanity
You will us all to be.   AMEN

Scripture Readings

Genesis 4:1–16   *Cain and Abel*
Genesis 45   *Joseph reveals himself*

Blessing

May you shape common ground
through love and generosity,
with your brother and sister
the world o'er.   AMEN

Parents

'Your people shall be my people,
and your God my God.'

~ Ruth 1:16 ~

Meditation

I, Naomi, who had brought two sons into the world,
watched over them as they grew,
married, settled, loved – then lost – life,
was now myself
lost, bereft, a child far from home.

Seeking intimacy,
I turned myself around,
to return to my people.

In my turning
she startled me,
this foreign wife of my boy,
this beautiful, loyal, trusting woman.
She, who had been neither,
became both daughter and parent
to me in my grief:

'Your people shall be my people,
and your God my God.'

Through her I learned the
godly art
of parenting as accompaniment:
she turned from the expected way,
valued me for all that I am,
walked with me to a strange land, and
loved me through it all.

As this 'daughter' adopted me,
I learned anew that I
was a beloved child of God.

Morning Prayer

Father–Mother God,
we pray for those who 'parent'
in expected, and unexpected ways.
On school runs and in nursing homes,
where we nurture children,
and 'parent' parents,
be our forever-companion.   AMEN

Evening Prayer

Dear God,
thank You for the day.
As we tuck in the little ones,
read to the sleepless,
and soothe the weary,
may Your love,
through our actions,
reach all in need of balm
tonight, and all nights.   AMEN

Scripture Readings

Ruth 1   *Ruth accompanies Naomi*
Matthew 19:29   *Leave brothers, sisters, parents,*
children for Jesus' sake

Blessing

The blessing of the God
who cares for all
and is companion to all
be with us this day and all days.   AMEN

Neighbours

'"To love Him with all the heart, and with all the understanding, and with all the strength", and "to love one's neighbour as oneself", – this is much more important than all whole burnt-offerings and sacrifices.'

~ Mark 12:33 ~

Meditation

People beside me, people before me.
A handful I know so well,
find so much with them in common,
but so many sharing my postcode, my car park,
my cafeteria – I share no more with than that.

There are some who are like me.
We've shared tea and biscuits,
even tears and laughter,
reinforcing each other for better and for worse.

There are some with whom the only view I share
is the one from our windows.
We quietly nod to acknowledge each other's existence
as we silently conspire to live lives next to each other
but never together.

There are some of whom I know only half a name;
the home behind their door,
the person behind their uniform,
bear a thousand imagined possibilities,
but the real neighbour, with real needs,
is dormant to my consciousness.

Morning Prayer

Lord Jesus, You moved into the neighbourhood
incarnate to us, ready and available to those in Your sights.
In the day before me, help me to draw nearer
to the people beside me and before me.

Help me to meet the needs I see before me,
whomsoever they belong to.
Help me to overcome
every barrier of 'us and them'
that I have erected in order to excuse myself
from loving in active sacrifice.

Help me to approach those near me
whom I do not know
with both confidence and compassion.
May the love I show to every neighbour this day
draw them nearer to Your kingdom.   AMEN

Evening Prayer

This evening I pray not for my refreshing, but theirs,
God, the neighbour whose brokenness I know better now.
Come and bind them up.

May You bring rest for the busy,
company for the lonely,
deliverance for the indebted,
renewal to the broken home,
salvation to those blind to You,
and daily bread for every table.

Let my neighbour come into Your kingdom, God.
AMEN

Scripture Readings

Mark 12:28–34   *Love your neighbour as yourself*
Luke 10:25–37   *Who is my neighbour?*

Blessing

O Master, grant that I may never seek
so much to be consoled as to console,
to be understood as to understand,
to be loved as to love with all my soul.   AMEN

~ adapted from the Peace Prayer of St Francis ~

Friends

'I have called you friends ...'

~ John 15:15 ~

Meditation

She was there at the school gate
that very first morning –
two five-year-olds meeting for the first time.
Now as adults, the best of friends.

We've laughed, we've cried,
we've laughed so much we've had to cry.
And I have been blessed
by her so many times along the way.

She is the one who does not judge,
who announces in action and in word:
'I am for you.'

And to know that God,
the Holy and Eternal One
calls me a friend.
What wondrous love is this?

This gift of grace
I gladly receive,
again and again.

Morning Prayer

I wonder at Your love,
I dwell in Your friendship,
I rest in Your peace.

As I embrace this day,
the places and the people around,
so let me also
offer Your embrace of love
to those I meet.

As I am known by You,
let me make You known.

Live in my laughter,
my work and my rest.
For in life and breath
I encounter You.   AMEN

Evening Prayer

I give thanks to You, O God,
my faithful companion,
for this day and all its moments.

I place into Your hands
any regrets, any hopes,
any worries, any fears.
You are like the best of friends –
You are with me
in good times and in bad.

I pray for those who feel alone,
and for those who are alone.
Let Your Spirit draw close,
with the blanket of Your love.   AMEN

Scripture Readings

Psalm 25:10–18   *The friendship of the Lord*
John 15:12–17   *Eternal friendship*

Blessing

In the company of God,
in the love of Christ,
in the peace of the Spirit,
I am held and known.   AMEN

Authorities

*'King Ahasuerus commanded Queen Vashti to be
brought before him, and she did not come.'*

~ Esther 1:17 ~

Meditation

There was a command.
There was disobedience.
The law is the law.
We are entrusted with the task of enforcing it.
We are the officials,
the authorities,
officially authorised to ensure the done thing
is done.
Because he is the king and she is his trophy.
He had filled his belly and wanted to fill his eyes
and show off his prize.
He has the right
because all power is in his hands,
not in hers,
no, not ever in hers.
Challenge us at your peril.
Disobey and you will pay the price.

She did not come.
The law is an ass
and she did not care for the ride.

Morning Prayer

Today, God, I will bow to much authority.
I will obey many laws.
Without thinking,
I will overstep no limits of accepted behaviour
and move within the bounds of civilised society.
I will be kept safe by responsibilities routinely
discharged,
orders sent down from above,
standards adhered to and regulations respected.

Help me to notice,
appreciate,
and show my gratitude today
towards people with authority
and people under authority,
doing what they are told,
visibly and invisibly creating order,
enhancing beauty,
easing difficulties.

Thank You, God,
for authority that enables,
power that equalises,
leadership that serves.   AMEN

Evening Prayer

Be with those who today and tomorrow
are working to show up unfair statutes,
rules that do not work for all,
policies with inherent prejudice.

Be with those who are disobeying with a clear conscience,
who are refusing a demand to be objectified,
who are listening to Your higher authority.

Be with those whose role is to govern
and infect any arrogance with restlessness
until it is a governing with grace.   AMEN

Scripture Readings

Esther 1:1–21   *Defying a king's command*
Jeremiah 19:14—20:6   *A clash of truth and lies*

Blessing

May we give our firm 'no'
to all that would dehumanise.
May we give our bold 'yes'
to all that commands us to act in love.
May we bend our knee gladly
to the rightful Governor of our souls.   AMEN

Them

But He passed through the midst of them.

~ Luke 4:30 ~

Meditation

Right in the midst of them.
That's where he is.
Tuts and ems on either side
are only to be expected
when words split open
comfortable creeds
and truth comes rolling forth
like a scroll unravelling.

Us and them
is not a must.
Division and discord leave us
in an empty place:
one where opinion splits
as quickly as a fickle crowd
and we come teetering to the edge
where our own demons wait to push.

We are all 'them';
all objects of a doing Word,
pre-positioned
to make sense of those around us,
related to others
despite our difference and our distance;
all gathered in one final sentence
which defeated death. Period.

Morning Prayer

Lord God,
for You each day was an opportunity
to meet people
in the rawness of their humanity
and to glimpse within them
something to love.

In the faithless You recognised need,
in the loveless You saw self-doubt,
in the outcast You witnessed a community
divided and conquered by fear of the different.

In our meeting of others today,
take us to the very edge of our understanding
that we may recognise in them our need for faith,
see in them our search for love
and witness through and to them
what it means to live in community.   AMEN

Evening Prayer

Thank You, Lord,
for walking in the midst of Your people today,
for noticing need when it passed me by,
for weeping at sorrow when my head was turned,
for holding out a hand when mine was hidden,
for understanding that I find it hard sometimes
not to make distinctions between myself and others.

Draw close this night, Lord,
that I may draw a line under today
and start afresh tomorrow.   AMEN

Scripture Readings

Luke 4:16–30   *Rejection of Jesus at Nazareth*
Galatians 3:26–29   *All children of God*

Blessing

To all God's children, peace,
within all God's children, love,
for all God's children, grace.
in all God's children, joy.   AMEN

Politicians

When Herod saw Jesus, he was very glad ...

~ Luke 23:8 ~

Meditation

What is to be seen
as the hand of welcome extends
and a conversation begins
on shared interest of events and issues,
personal, local and worldwide?
Awestruck,
for a moment one is silent,
bewildered at the power
that could be wielded.

In the pattern of society
the politician's voice is the bold colour
that can blend
and reveal the hidden hints of others
or contrast,
clashing with all that sits around.
As the personal warmth engages,
the listening ear
and the passion for people
dispel the uncertainty,
and shared humanity allows for diverse opinion
to craft perspectives and policies.

Hopefully,
as conversation ends,
each party has been heard
and the ambition for community health pursued.

Morning Prayer

Prince of Peace,
we would all like to think
that when faced with injustice,
we would speak up for those who are being belittled,

and stand on the side of right.
It should be a clear-cut choice.
We give thanks for those who engage in decision-making
in the hope of shaping and restoring our communities.
Principles come in shades of grey,
not always black or white,
and so we seek forgiveness
for the shirking of responsibility
and avoidance of the issue,
hoping that the Counsellor
will guide our thoughts and actions
to make You present to those who are to be lifted up.
AMEN

Evening Prayer

When political decisions made this day
have sided with the powerful,
may a challenging voice speak out.
Lord of the dusk and the dawn,
while the frustration of the wrong happening
may need to be put to bed this night,
may the dreams of possibility
stir active plans for change
so that Christ's compelling call
to search for those in need
arises with the morning.   AMEN

Scripture Readings

Luke 23:6–12   *Jesus is taken to Herod*
1 Kings 18:16–21   *Ahab meets Elijah*

Blessing

Mighty God, reign in our hearts,
Prince of Peace, uphold us in justice,
Wonderful Counsellor, guide us in this time.   AMEN

Enemies

They beset me with words of hate,
and attack me without cause.

~ Psalm 109:3 ~

Meditation

The saliva drips down my cheek.
My lips are held tight, but I can taste the salt
of the spittle of hatred.
I don't know who spat at me –
an ocean of faces are before me.
The din of insults makes me dizzy,
a cacophony of crowing.
The waving fists of swastika-branded arms
threaten to knock me out.

And yet I stand proud,
linked arm in arm
with my brothers and sisters in Christ,
rubbing salt into the wounds of fascism.

Lamb of God, who takes away the sins of the world,
have mercy on us.

(This meditation is written from the experience of the multi-denominational clergy who gathered in Charlottesville, USA, linking arms to offer peaceful protest and witness in August 2017)

Morning Prayer

This is the day,
this is the day that the Lord has made.
Let us be salt and light and leaven.
Let us respond to hatred and anger and envy
with love.
Let us be the people You call us to be,
even when faced with those who treat us as enemies.

Lamb of God, who takes away the sins of the world,
have mercy on us.   AMEN

Evening Prayer

When terror threatens to engulf us,
when machine guns and knives are wielded,
and cars are driven intentionally to kill,
let us know that this is not Your way.

Keep us in Your presence,
and strengthen us to work for justice and for peace
to bring about Your kingdom here on earth.

This night, and in the new morning,
Lamb of God,
who takes away the sins of the world,
have mercy on us.   AMEN

Scripture Readings

Luke 6:27–36   *Love your enemies*
Psalm 109   *Acts of David's enemies*

Blessing

Do justice.
Love kindly.
Walk humbly with God.
This day, and every day.
Be blessed.   AMEN

Strangers

'Lord, when was it that we saw You hungry or thirsty or a stranger or naked or sick or in prison, and did not take care of You?'

~ Matthew 25:44 ~

Meditation

Was it You, Lord, in that stranger,
and only now I realise it?
Was it You, Lord, in those chance encounters,
that made my day, or made me think,
or simply made me smile?
That encouraged or comforted me?
Or even changed my life?
We may never know the person's name,
but we'll always remember
how they made us feel.

Is it You, Lord, in the person whose
life experience differs from mine?
For I may have something to learn,
or receive, or become.
Perhaps, perhaps, You might even use me
to be a blessing to a stranger?
I don't want You to be a stranger to me.

You were always stopping for strangers,
the sick, the seeker, the desperate,
the hungry, the angry, the anxious,
to answer questions, to heal,
and point to the kingdom of God.

And like the couple walking to Emmaus,
You came alongside, even when
they were going in the wrong direction.

*'Often, often, often goes the Christ
in the stranger's guise.'*

~ *Celtic Rune of Hospitality* ~

Morning Prayer

Your grace is new every morning,
and my gratitude is new every morning.
May I be as gracious to strangers
as I am to loved ones,
and as gracious to loved ones
as I am to strangers.

Lord, who do You want to love,
through me, today?   AMEN

Evening Prayer

I remember before You, Lord Jesus,
all the people I met today ...

and I ask Your blessing on each one.

Now, in confidence, I place them,
and myself, and all my loved ones,
wherever they may be,
into Your eternal safekeeping.   AMEN

Scripture Readings

Matthew 25:31–46   *'I was a stranger'*
James 2:1-5   *Appearances can deceive*

Blessing

Stay with us, Lord, for it is toward evening,
and the day is far spent.
Be with us with Thy grace and bounty,
with Thy holy word and sacrament.
Remain with us and with Thy whole church
through time and eternity.   AMEN

Refugees

*Then Joseph got up, took the child and His mother
by night ...*

~ Matthew 2:14 ~

Meditation

The nine lessons and carols have found new life
and meaning, echoing in frequent media coverage
of parents bundling weary children
with blankets, fear and hope,
carried over hostile borders
in the wee small hours of the night.
Escaping the brutality of a regime
ruled by violence and cruelty.
Spending formative years
far from home in a country
that enslaved ancestors
who went on a long wandering exodus,
refugees weave throughout this story
that has become our story.

Did Joseph manage to work,
with his tools being back in Nazareth?
Did Mary worry about her baby's future every day?
Did they manage to get past the language barrier?
Were they able to let loved ones know where they were?
And were they welcomed as neighbours,
with the realisation that with every refugee
we re-encounter the vulnerability of incarnation,
we lock eyes with the image of the divine?

Morning Prayer

Refugee Jesus,
grant strength to those weary with travelling;
grant hope to those who are stuck in-between;
grant comfort to those separated from family;
grant healing to those living with trauma;

grant provision for those made destitute again;
grant wisdom and compassion to decision makers;
grant tenacity and companions to those who journey on.
Grant us the encounters to welcome and offer hospitality
to those who are far from home.   AMEN

Evening Prayer

We pray for all those who,
instead of brushing their teeth,
are packing a bag with supplies,
waking tired children
and are bundling their lives into cars or
pulling on shoes, finally taking to the road,
not knowing if they will ever return home.

We pray for those who cannot sleep,
who live with anxiety and trauma,
stuck in refugee camps or awaiting asylum;
for those who refuse to be comforted,
their worst fears already realised;
and for those who did not manage to escape,
who could not afford to become refugees.

We pray for them 'peace beyond all understanding',
and we pray for the peace of heaven on earth.   AMEN

Scripture Readings

Matthew 2:9–20   *A family escape in the night*
Psalm 36:5–9   *All people may take refuge*

Blessing

May God bless us with encounters
that turn strangers into neighbours,
that turn fear into friendships,
that turn hatred into hospitality,
that turn pain into peace.   AMEN

Those Who Serve Us

'She said, "Please let me glean and gather among the sheaves behind the reapers." So she came, and she has been on her feet from early this morning until now, without resting even for a moment.'

~ Ruth 2:7 ~

Meditation

Look at Ruth,
her faithful commitment, selfless loyalty
and loving kindness.
Her service transforms Naomi's emptiness and despair
to a fulsomeness and joy.
Humble.
Vigilant, awake, seeing the needs of others.
Fully present and genuine in her love.
Gleaning and gathering remnants that would suffice.

In a common standing,
a web of serving one another.
My neighbour has much to offer me.
Both are free to give and receive
in a relationship of mutual benefit – serving.

Morning Prayer

Remind me throughout this day
of the humble gleaner
and others who, in their faithful commitment,
in vulnerable, humble, loving acts of sacrifice
serve me, serve others.
Too often I confess taking them for granted,
not even acknowledging the person,
in my hurry, blind to the small acts of kindness.
Remove my pride and blindness to see
those who serve me …
to the kindnesses …
to the care and attention …

In each seemingly incidental circumstance and encounter,
where transformations occur,
make me thankful and help me speak words of blessing,
even in a simple *'Thank you'*.
Open the door to Your blessings in this day.   Amen

Evening Prayer

In gleaning through this day I recall Your presence, Lord.
Lord, help me to look at my day with Your eyes,
not merely my own.
I come Lord to thank You for the gift of this day.
In gratitude I bless You for …

Guided by the Holy Spirit I sift through the day.
I notice the joys of the day,
no matter how small or insignificant they might appear.
I notice those who have served me, blessed me …

Holy Spirit, bring to my attention
what has been significant today in these encounters.
Reveal to me what insight and understandings
You have to show me.

I ask for what I need for tomorrow to walk humbly.
Amen

Scripture Readings

| | Ruth 2 | *A humble gleaner* |
| Matthew 23:11–12 | *To be a servant* |

Blessing

The Lord repay you for what you have done,
and a full reward be given you by the Lord God,
under whose wings you have come to take refuge!
Amen

Cold Callers

'Be not forgetful to entertain strangers ...'
~ Hebrews 13:2 (KJV) ~

Meditation

Cold callers.
That ring of the doorbell or the telephone,
that person on the street with a clipboard or tablet:
'Just a few questions ...'
'Not trying to sell you anything ...'
'Who supplies your gas and gullibility?'

But be not forgetful to entertain
the pitch,
the plea,
the jingle on repeat,
for thereby some have entertained angels unawares.
We are unprepared
for strangers
and strangeness,
for encounters with others
that veer off from the expected.

Jesus' ministry was spent amongst
tax collectors, beggars, and shady characters,
chancers who spoke at the wrong time
and who said the wrong thing.
Blue sky thinking needs clouds of interruption.
So bless the disruption
and bless the disrupter,
for thereby some have entertained angels.

Morning Prayer

Dear God,
in a world of cold callers,
help us to be warm listeners,
open to encounter,
open to others.
Give us opportunities
today
to act on this openness,
to be vulnerable
and hopeful
and welcoming.   AMEN

Evening Prayer

Dear God,
we pray for wisdom in tackling the systems
that make us cold to one another,
suspicious of one another,
fearful of one another.

Instead of swords,
perhaps we can beat our call centre headsets
into ploughshares?   AMEN

Scripture Readings

Hebrews 13   *Advice for living*
Isaiah 2:1–4   *A vision of peace*

Blessing

Bless us, God,
with Your warmth and wisdom,
as we entertain strangers
and entertain the possibility of encounter.   AMEN

Church Folk

Some proclaim Christ from envy and rivalry,
but others from goodwill.

~ Philippians 1:15 ~

Meditation

What a mixed bunch we are!

With the right sort of encouragement,
we rally round and commit to new projects,
more easily if they will improve church buildings.
Even then we have such mixed feelings,
lamenting the past like the older folk of Ezra's day,
struggling with the new,
but usually ready to enjoy anniversaries
and cheer new landmarks.

However, if our leader gets under pressure,
or hits a crisis, then we soon divide up –
some for, some against;
we keep doing the same old things,
but with such mixed motives.
And this seems to be as true in keen new churches
as in easy-going traditional ones.

The coming of Christ has not changed human nature,
but without Him we could not have the 'someday'
that the Spirit holds before us.

Morning Prayer

Today we name our leaders before You …
May they know when and how to present new ideas,
and also discover the marvel of finding better ideas
arising from their people.

Today we remember the older folk in our churches,
who know the God present at their beginning …
May they discover the God present in their future,
and the future of their congregation.

Today we pray for younger people
who may need to discover You present in the church,
as in the world they live in daily ...
May they find a garden growing within their lives,
a garden where You are tending the trees. AMEN

Evening Prayer

O God, grant us to know that it is not the beginning
of any great work, but the continuing of it
till it be thoroughly finished,
which yields the true glory.

~ *A prayer attributed to Sir Francis Drake* ~

Gracious God, imaginative and patient,
we are glad that so many people trust Your steadfast
love, which persists for Israel and for the whole world.

We are glad that Christ has been proclaimed today,
in the words of prophets and evangelists
risking their freedom,
in the lives of church folk
seeking to bear witness to Whose they are,
and Whom they serve.

We are glad that You have laid
a great foundation in our lives;
we seek Your help to build with good material
that will stand all tests;
we trust Your Spirit to complete all You desire for us,
and for those whom we love.   AMEN

Scripture Readings

Ezra 3:10–13   *The founding of a new temple*
Philippians 1:12–18   *Paul is realistic about motives*

Blessing

May you know the purity of an undivided heart.
May you know the zeal of a disciplined spirit.
May you know the direction of Christ
and seek His honour.   AMEN

ENCOUNTERS
WITH THE WORLD

O Lord, how manifold are Your works!
In wisdom You have made them all

~ Psalm 104:24 ~

Thresholds

'I would rather be a doorkeeper in the house of my God ...'

~ Psalm 84:10 ~

Meditation

Nothing is instant.
No photograph, coffee, or message
is instant.
No starter's pistol, flare, or alarm
is instant.
No connecting blow, glance, or fall
is instant.
No sound wave, light particle, or physical sensation
is instant.

There is latency everywhere,
the gap between things,
little liminal thresholds,
where light hits the eye,
sound hooks the ear,
and touch brushes the skin.
When we witness the world,
we are part of the circuit of creation,
feeling its current –
the colours,
sounds,
and vibrations
existing between us and what we see,
hear,
or feel.

Morning Prayer

Dear God,
This day help us to notice and
experience and
celebrate and
delight in
the wonder of Your creation.   AMEN

Evening Prayer

Dear God,
You rejoice in the inhabited world
and we rejoice in it.
Bind us closer to our environment,
to one another.
Wrap us up in it,
bundle us up in it,
hold us close in it,
as we stand on the threshold,
doorkeepers in Your house. AMEN

Scripture Readings

Psalm 84	*Doorkeeper in God's house*
Hebrews 3:1–6	*The builder of all things is God*

Blessing

God, we ask for You to be with us
as we stand on the
threshold,
the precipice,
the edge,
between what we know
and what we don't.   AMEN

Weather

You set the beams of Your chambers on the waters,
You make the clouds Your chariot,
You ride on the wings of the wind ...

~ Psalm 104:3 ~

Meditation

Oh how we moan about the weather,
the source of our life and living!

Without weather, no crops;
without crops, no food;
without food, no survival.
Teach us to celebrate
the power of the weather
to bring us life.

Weather gives me language to understand myself:
a grey day, much thick cloud,
a sense of getting nowhere, a nothing day;
a bright, exciting, clear sky of a day, open horizons,
a sense of posssiblity, the feeling of fulfilment.
Weather empowers my inner world,
gives me texture to describe, to talk with myself,
with God – about what it is like inside.
Jesus said *'Consider the lilies of the fields'* ...
they get what they need to grow.
And so maybe our inner weather
is giving us what we need to grow?

Teach me, Creator God,
to hear You through the weather –
without and within, as Jesus did.

Morning Prayer

Loving, parenting, nurturing God,
help me listen right now to my experience of the weather,
my inner reality, as well as the outside world.

Enable me to tune into both weathers –
and the stillness and stability of Your love,
solid as a mountain, beautiful and flexible as a tree,
present, and holding me, and all I need to be.

From that still place,
enable me to tune into the weather,
to listen to it in a way that gives me energy,
to be creative with what is around and within me;
that I may know myself
as part of Your unfolding creation –
day by day and moment by moment.   AMEN

Evening Prayer

Creator of the inner and outer weather,
as I look back on this day,
help me appreciate what has been
the ebb and flow of my emotional weather,
the demands or delights of the physical weather.

O Creative One,
may You keep speaking to me through all weathers.
May Your Spirit work in me as I sleep.
May I enter the dark with trust
that You are restoring me,
resting in me and with me,
to create a new day.   AMEN

Scripture Readings

Psalm 104   *Seeing God's works through nature*
Philippians 4:11–13   *Being content in all circumstances*

Blessing

May the Creator of light and dark,
sunshine and rain, breeze and storm,
refresh and remake you,
create within you
the capacity to greet
the weather of tomorrow.   AMEN

Animals

My beloved is like a gazelle ... Look, there he stands ...
gazing in at the windows ...

~ Song of Solomon 2:9 ~

Meditation

It's not the first time that we have met
at this time of the morning.
Each time we meet
we surprise each other
as we run almost head on to stand opposed.
The speed with which we move contrasts,
for you are lithe and sleek,
moving gracefully across the fields,
the valleys and hills almost levelled
by the movement of your limbs.
Meanwhile I stand puffing breathlessly,
half relieved to get a break
from the pounding of the pavement,
but equally transfixed by the beauty of your form.

As our eyes meet,
we share the fear of not knowing
what the other will do next.
You are ready to leap forth,
golden flesh quivering with energy.

Then a noise disturbs our moment,
and you nimbly bound across the boundary,
and I can only stand and watch
the power of your frame pulse towards the horizon,
before you are lost within the camouflage
of grass and tree.

Morning Prayer

Creator of all,
what diversity and wonder
You have made in flesh and fur,
scale and shell,
feather and hide.
Each unique form equally unique in habit and trait,
and need of care.

We have been gifted with the stewardship of all around
and in our hands You have placed
the responsibility to marvel and ensure
each part of the creation is valued, loved and treasured.
May each moment of this day respect
the precious life You gave.   AMEN

Evening Prayer

Let us rejoice in bird and bee,
in cat, dog, cow and horse,
in lion, elephant and giraffe,
in fish, dolphin and crocodile
as their colours and traits
shape the world You made for us to share.
And while I might not be so keen on snakes,
or wasps, or spiders, or woodlice,
may I find them wonderful too
for they were given by You.   AMEN

Scripture Readings

Song of Solomon 2:3–13   *A celebration of love*
Genesis 2:18–20   *Companionship for humanity*

Blessing

In the chorus of the dawn,
in the splashing of the seas,
in the rumble of the jungle,
may the voice of God reveal
the changing pattern of creation.   AMEN

Mountains

How beautiful upon the mountains ...

~ Isaiah 52:7 ~

Meditation

When I reach the peak,
catch my breath and stand on the summit,
I sense the grandeur in the ancient –
in the landscape that speaks of time.

When I wonder at formations
beneath my feet,
I am reminded of my infancy
in the life of the world.

What does it mean
to be before and after time?
What does it mean
to be everlasting?
I see mystery and majesty
in the Eternal.
In God.

Let me gaze upon Your beauty
in mountains and Munros,
in glens and gullies,
in all that speaks of You
this and every day.

Morning Prayer

In You O God, I am at home.
I join with generations before
and find that You are the place
in which I dwell.

On lofty peaks, and in deepest valleys,
You are the God who is with me.
In the unfolding of this day,
I know You within and around me.

Let Your Spirit bring life,
that my life may point to You,
as the peaks reach to the sky.   AMEN

Evening Prayer

As light casts its shadow on this day,
I have known You at my rising,
and You are with me still.

I praise You, Christ,
for You have announced peace
and shared Your good news with me.
You invite me to the mountain top of faith
where I can dwell with You.

In the evening light,
I offer my thanksgiving
for the blessings of this day.

I call to mind
the moments of darkness I have known,
praying for those experiencing wilderness
and for all who long for Your love.

Unite me in faith,
with all Your people.
In every place.   AMEN

Scripture Readings

Psalm 90   *God's eternity*
Isaiah 52:7–10   *Joy all around*

Blessing

On the journey,
in the twists and turns,
and on the mountain top,
You are always blessing Your people.
I am at home in You.   AMEN

Valleys

God is bringing you into a good land ... with springs ... welling up in valleys.

~ Deuteronomy 8:7 ~

Meditation

Sinai desert valley –
floor of dust between my toes;
walls of sandstone rising east and west.
Roof of shimmering blue by day,
black velvet by night,
studded with six thousand stars.
Cradled between golden heights,
windworn rock of patterned ripples,
warm beneath my palms and cheek,
cool in the clefts where I sit and gaze,
and sit for timeless hours and gaze ...

Waterless place
that drenched and quenched my deepest thirst;
walls that opened up a rare expanse of freedom;
sifting sand that restored my solid ground.

Silence of the Creator's song,
soundless ringing of sacred joy,
emptiness filling me to overflowing.
Desert valley – summit
of divine contentment.

Morning Prayer

Dear God,
I remember the lessons –
u-shaped, v-shaped, hanging;
glaciers, rivers, meanders.
I remember their becoming real
way beyond the classroom –
wooded slopes and flat scrub,
winding streams and raging rivers,
high hillsides and lost views.

Today, some are needing the shelter and peace of the glen.
Some know the vulnerability
of their home between the hills.
Some are walking in the shadow of death,
the dark vale of tears.
Some are looking up in longing for the mountains,
seeing only concrete towers.
You know the troughs and canyons of all our experience.
Lead us and protect us this day,
holding us in the hollow of Your hand.   Amen

Evening Prayer

God, may I lie down tonight
as in a green and fertile valley.
May rest come as to a seasoned hiker,
stopping where gurgling water dances over mossy stones.
The path upward
is not always the best to follow.
The high place
is not always the prize to chase.
Lush meadows and quiet streams are here
in the dips and the dells.
Time to rest.
Time for sleep.
Your good gifts, gentle God,
generously given,
gratefully received.   Amen

Scripture Readings

Deuteronomy 8:1–10   *A good land to live in*
Deuteronomy 34:1–8   *A good land to die in*

Blessing

Where water and ice have sculpted the way,
may God's good land hold us and speak to us –
heights and depths carved as surely
as our names upon God's hand.   Amen

Desert

'I have commanded the ravens to feed you there.'

~ 1 Kings 17:4 ~

Meditation

The uncommon ground.
A geography of abandonment;
no landmarks to guide our way.
All seems removed.
A spirituality of imperfection.
A way of cleansing.
Entry into what is unnerving,
uncovering sins, limits,
confronting deep fears, desires.
Feelings of abandonment and loneliness.
Learning the painful process of letting go.
The desert loves to strip bare the familiar.
Yet there … encounter with God.

The call comes 'Go and hide' in a *desert* place.
Wait in the silence beyond words;
it is there that illumination comes,
solace, nourishment for the soul;
waiting for God to break in,
God's provision bringing newness,
opening up the way to life again.

Morning Prayer

Heavenly Father, at Your bidding,
I commit to sit in silence;
To sit honestly with the stillness, the waves of emotion,
however unexpected, that arise.
And so to be attentive to You, Lord,
to be present with You in solitude and silence.

Lord God, prepare me for the way ahead.
Reveal to me the passions, temptations
and inner wilderness of my life.

Exposed to my imperfections,
may I let go of all that darkens and hinders.
Cleanse me and renew me
in this rough wild place.
May I find nourishment for my soul,
healing from contentment in You alone.

Teach me to live with myself,
that in this day
I may learn to give myself fully in love for others,
To love sacrificially, seeking nothing in return.   AMEN

Evening Prayer

Heavenly Father, I come to the silence,
the daughter of patience,
the mother of watchfulness.
I hide myself in You, as I abandon my words,
allow new awareness to come.
Awaken me from numbness to the world around me,
from the dullness of my vision …

I surrender myself to You, Lord, in the silence
a way of waiting,
a way of watching,
a way of noticing
what is going on in my heart and in the world.

Scripture Readings

> 1 Kings 17:1–6   *Elijah fed*
> Luke 4:1–13   *Jesus in the desert*

Blessing

> In the desert place of struggles,
> may the Lord make you truly alive,
> and the amazing grace of Jesus Christ
> be with your spirit.   AMEN

Encounters with the World

Water

The Samaritan woman said to Him, 'How is it that you,
a Jew, ask a drink of me, a woman of Samaria?'
(Jews do not share things in common with Samaritans.)

~ John 4:9 ~

Meditation

In our parched lives
for what do we thirst?
Forgiveness?
Peace?
Opportunity?
Reconciliation?
Acceptance?
Love?

The Woman of Samaria met Jesus at a well.
He was thirsty, but had nothing with which to get water.
The woman's thirst was deeper.
Jesus tells the woman of the Living Water He could provide;
a greater thirst quenched.

Where might we encounter the Living Water?
Who is Jesus?
What needs will Jesus satisfy?
Having encountered Jesus by the water,
will you, like the woman of Samaria,
be emboldened to lead others
to encounter Him?

Morning Prayer

Living Water,
in this morning hour,
when the sun is rising
and the world is wet with dew,
rain down Your blessings on us once more,
and prepare us to encounter You and Yours
by wells of living water,
in cafés, halls and kitchens.

Teach us to cup our hands
and graciously share with one another and with You,
souls invigorated, lives fruitful,
drenched in the Water of Life,
through Jesus Christ our Lord. AMEN

Evening Prayer

Living Water,
whether this day has been as dry as dust,
or flooded with life-giving grace,
now we lie down.
Whether this day has reminded us
of our fluid baptised lives,
or the arid spaces of our cracked souls,
now we lie down.
Bring us to the well of sleep,
where in its depths we may be refreshed,
and made ready for the coming dawn.
Bring us promise of renewing water,
and places where, through stream and river,
sea and ocean,
the mighty water of Your restless love
may wash over us
and cleanse us for new days,
and further meeting with You
and with Your friends,
in Christ's Name we pray.   AMEN

Scripture Readings

Genesis 1:1–2   *Encounter with creation*
John 4:1–30   *Encounter with Living Water*

Blessing

In the water of baptism, find new life;
in the water of life, find new strength;
that in your beginning and in your ending,
you may be borne up on the endless stream
of Christ's unfailing love and blessing.   AMEN

Moor

O sing to the Lord a new song;
sing to the Lord, all the earth.

~ Psalm 96:1 ~

Meditation

> *'A humble scene in a backward place*
> *Where no one important ever looked*
> *The raving flowers looked up in the face*
> *Of the One and the Endless . . . [where]*
> *beautiful, beautiful, beautiful God*
> *Was breathing His love by a cut-away bog.'*

– *Patrick Kavanagh*

While Kavanagh was still waiting
for his family inheritance of moorland,
he moved to Dublin.
Paul, waiting for a greater inheritance,
said to his friends at Corinth, *'All things belong to you'*.

How could he say that?
Well, Paul had just said that we are God's temple,
and Jews had known since the Exile
that the earth was made to be God's temple,
so he was just putting two and two together
– a logical move, which enables us to bring
the whole creation to God in prayer.

Morning Prayer

Mouse-ear and orchid, praise the Lord.
Heather and blaeberry, praise the Lord.
Clubmoss and bedstraw, praise the Lord.
Sphagnum and willowherb, praise the Lord.
Praise Him and magnify Him for ever.

Today, most lovely Lord,
I seek Your presence in the wild moorland of my living.
Make my life a song of praise
at the heart of all You have made. AMEN

Evening Prayer

Tonight let me walk the moors that have enfolded
my life ... the wild places that have scared me ...
in which I got lost for a while ...
the beautiful landscapes that have enthralled me
and held me spell-bound ...
the surprising journeys that have challenged me
and shaped my life in ways I did not expect ...

Tonight let me think of others abroad on wild moors ...
may they find You there to guide them,
and to give them shelter.

Tonight let me think of the world of nature ...
may it find protection,
may those who treat it as spoil be frustrated,
may those who love it be encouraged.

Triune God, You have wonderfully shared
Your inner beauty with us in Christ.
You have invited us to see the wild moorland of
experience as a place where You are at home,
and to see the gentle valleys of ordinary life
as a place where the untamed freedom of Your being
can meet us and transform us.   AMEN

Scripture Readings

Psalm 96   *Let the whole earth praise God*
1 Corinthians 3:16–23   *How a triune God ties up all things*

Blessing

May the green scallop of marsh pennywort
    be your comfort.
May the bright yellow of bog asphodel
    be your treasure.
May the firm pattern of fern and fescue
    give your life meaning,
and the gentle embrace of Father, Son and Spirit
    grant you all things.   AMEN

Trees

For the healing of the nations

~ Revelation 22:2 ~

Meditation

Branches to climb.
Twigs to float.
Seeds to twirl.
Conkers to crack.
Sticks to throw.
Fruit to pick.
Roots that trip.
Trunks to hide behind.
Shelter to surround.
Shade to cool.
Wood for fire.
Rings to count.
Trees to encounter.

A strong and solid presence.
A pliable and flexible resistance.
A surging and recycling energy.
An annual seasonal resurrection.

From the garden to the city, trees provide
shade for visiting strangers;
lessons for frustrated prophets;
food for aliens, orphans and widows;
wood for mangers and crosses;
leaves to cover shame and
leaves to heal the nations
and the wounds of our souls.

Morning Prayer

Today we give thanks for trees, God,
for their harmonious breath,
for their cycle of life,
for their shade and shelter,
for their provision and presence,
for their symbolism and endurance,
for their rootedness and poise.

May we go out into today with joy
and be led back at its end in peace.
May we remain rooted in Your Word
and stretch into the gaps and the light.
And with the trees of field may we
clap our hands in praise of the
wonderful works of Your hands.   AMEN

Evening Prayer

As the leaves of the trees curl up
with diminishing light,
we turn in at the end of today,
sheltered by Your peace,
surrounded by Your protection,
resting in Your presence.
Renew us with restorative sleep.
Heal us with nature's balm.
Thanks be to God.   AMEN

Scripture Readings

Isaiah 55:12–13	*The trees clap their hands*
Revelation 22:1–7	*The tree of life for healing*

Blessing

May your faith overcome worry,
as a seedling breaks through the soil.
May your hope move into resistance,
as a sapling grows into a tree.
May your love reach out to embrace,
as branches stretch into the light.   AMEN

Cave

He came to a cave, and spent the night there.

~ 1 Kings 19:9 ~

Meditation

Sometimes it is in the hidden
that nature unveils her greatest beauty.
Weathered rocks
unearth patterns of a past age.
Down damp walls
trickle secrets yet to be exposed.
Cracks and crevices
hide stories never told.
Dark corners
shroud ancient mysteries.

Safety and refuge, come wind, earthquake, fire.

Sometimes it is in the hidden
that creation unveils her greatest treasure.
A stone rolled away
reveals a blueprint for the future.
Dried up hope
gives way to living water.
Fresh truths creep through
fractured faith.
Light and life
burst in to disperse shadows.

And a voice breaks through the silence.

Morning Prayer

How tempting, Lord,
to stay in bed today
and hide beneath the covers.
How easy to close the door
against the world
and take refuge in the haven of my home.

But You won't pass me by.
You rouse me from my refuge
for there is work to do.
Speak to me today.
Remind me I am not alone
when sheltered in Your love.   AMEN

Evening Prayer

How tempting, Lord,
to go to bed tonight
and forget all I have seen and heard today.
How easy to close the door
against the needs of the world
and take refuge in my own well-being.

Yet I cannot pass by those
who rouse my concern
so there is work to do.
Speak to them tonight, I pray.
Remind them they are not alone
when sheltered in Your love.   AMEN

Scripture Readings

1 Kings 19:9–13   *Elijah meets God at Horeb*
John 11:38–44   *Raising of Lazarus*

Blessing

May God's light seek you.
May God's hand reach you.
May God's voice speak to you.
May God's grace gather you.
May God's love enfold you.
May God's strength be your refuge.   AMEN

City

*But seek the welfare of the city where I have sent you
into exile, and pray to the Lord on its behalf, for in its
welfare you will find your welfare.*

~ Jeremiah 29:7 ~

Meditation

Hustle and bustle. Jostle and tussle.
Bright and busy. Full and fast.
A day at the office, a night on the town.
Light, noise, movement,
and most of all … people.
So many people.

This place envelops me
Where nothing is still, neither am I.
Senses assaulted … I'm drinking it all up.
This place is a bubble of distraction,
a hub of personal interaction,
the insatiable pursuit of satisfaction.

But most of all … people.
So many people.
How will God's voice be heard clear and resounding
amid the noise?
How will the kingdom rise amongst the towers?
How will anonymous crowds see a king in their midst?

Morning Prayer

Lord Almighty,
I get so caught up with my corner, my comforts.
Help me to see the city that You've drawn me to
with Your concern and Your compassion.

May the chatter never distract me from Your voice.
May I hide not in the crowds but in Christ.

Show me
what You beckon me to notice through the noise,

where You tell me to turn and walk
against the city's flow,
and where You tell me to run
along with the breathless.

May I be to this city, and it to me,
a blessing, not a curse.   AMEN

Evening Prayer

I pray for the prosperity of this city,
that Your people here might help it flourish
and that we might flourish with it.

Let the city increase.
Let there be jobs. Let there be justice.
Let there be good government.
Let there be safety. Let there be beauty.
Let there be planning authorised by the Author.
Let there be schools. Let there be community.
Let there be a greenhouse for young life to thrive.
Let there be care. Let there be service.
Let there be provision for the fragile in the incessant pace.

As the city sleeps, watch over it.
May it wake each new day with new hope and new life.
AMEN

Scripture Readings

Jeremiah 29:1–14   *Flourishing the earthly city*
Revelation 21:1–5   *Expecting the heavenly city*

Blessing

The Lord grant you peace and prosperity
as He grants it to your city.
The Lord cause you to increase.
The Lord give you patience in exile.
The Lord lift your eyes to see
that city to which you are truly citizen
descend upon you.   AMEN

Traffic Jam

But Your wrath has come, and the time for ...
destroying those who destroy the earth.

~ Revelation 11:18 ~

Meditation

I sit here on the gridlocked bypass
most nights after work.
Brake lights filtered through rivulets of rain
efficiently swept away by the tireless wipers,
only to return, for a brief moment.

Swept away again.
I feel imprisoned
in this cage of steel and plastic.
The salesman sold me on the notion
that it was the most
carbon neutral car on the road
A good, environmental choice.
Yet, I sit here, alone,
in choked lanes of single drivers,
all imprisoned by the evening commute.

I get tired, sitting in that traffic jam.
The air should be still and clear,
but the revving of engines to stop 'that man'
from cutting in down the hard shoulder
chokes the air and filters through the car's vents.

The fumes rise up, a yellow vapour
enveloping the city's atmospheric rims,
like the tidal mark of scum round a bathtub.
The whole of creation cries out
as pollution's drug silently kills us all.

Oh God, what have we done?

Morning Prayer

God of the new day,
perhaps I have never properly considered
how I should actively care for Your earth.
Maybe I have thought
that it is for someone else to do,
or that my small acts have no bearing.
Forgive me Lord.
Help me to do better this day. AMEN

Evening Prayer

Did I drive today when I could have walked?
Did I tip my rubbish in the general bin
instead of sorting the recycling piece by piece?
Did I leave the work computer on overnight?
Did I throw on a jumper or did I turn up the thermostat?
Did I leave the hot water running needlessly?
Did I buy another plastic bag instead of reusing
my 'bag for life'?
Did I choose to be gentle on Your earth?

Only You and I truly know
the answers to these questions.
Help me to do better tomorrow.   AMEN

Scripture Readings

Hebrews 1	*Reflecting the glory of the Creator God*
Revelation 11:15–19	*The kingdom of the world becomes God's kingdom*

Blessing

Walk gently on this earth;
touch the world lightly;
choose wisely;
as the blessings of God are all around you.
God's kingdom is near.   AMEN

Phone Box

'Ask, and it will be given to you ...'

~ Matthew 7:7 ~

Meditation

At the fork of a road
on the edge of Loch Gorm
on the Isle of Islay
where a lonely road comes from Sanaigmore
another from Loch Gruinart
and the third from Saligo,
in the middle of nowhere
in all its bright redness
against the marram gold
and clover green,
stands a phone box
that connects nowhere
to everywhere:
Islay to Damascus,
Aden,
Juba:
a global highway
on the back roads of Islay.

If only these worried cities could know
they are connected
to the peace of that junction
by that phone box
now waiting for their call.

Morning Prayer

May this day be filled with connections
to people I have never met;
a voice, real and alive,
rather than a digital string,
that savours the moment
and shapes the sound,
the sound,

the sound,
of my name,
as I reply with theirs,
held and honoured by my voice
that speaks such poetry
into the noise of the world. AMEN

Evening Prayer

As I reflect on the day,
I pause at the times
where I have left You as 'caller waiting';
where the pips have rushed me
and our conversation has ended unfinished;
where circumstances and pain
have been 'unable to connect' us today.
In this evening time
may I make that call
and listen for Your voice,
Your love,
and Your grace
calling me.   AMEN

Scripture Readings

Matthew 7:7–11   *Ask, seek, knock*
Isaiah 40:6–9   *A voice to the cities*

Blessing

When the moment comes,
may you find that connecting place
where the noise of the world
is answered with the peace of God.   AMEN

ENCOUNTERS
WITH JESUS

Suddenly Jesus met them and said, 'Greetings!'
And they came to Him, took hold of His feet,
and worshipped Him.

~ Matthew 28:9 ~

Would-be Disciple

'Then come, follow me ...'

~ Mark 10:21 ~

Meditation

'You lack one thing,' He said,
and my world fell apart.
How could I respond to all He asked?
It was too much.

Entering my comfortable space,
making demands of me –
Is this really what faith
and following is about?

Yet Jesus looks and asks
only in love.
I must not miss His tender gaze,
or I might turn away.

So let me ask my questions,
that I might hear God's wisdom.
For He invites me every day
to encounter Him anew.

Morning Prayer

Living Spirit,
You are as breath to me.
You are present before I know it,
and fill my life with good things.

Let me begin this day with praise,
for You are my God.
I praise You my Creator,
for I am beloved in Christ,
and guided by Your Spirit.   AMEN

Evening Prayer

My thoughts and prayers rise to You,
the One who is Eternal.

You have known my questions,
my fears, my anxieties,
and have met with me in Christ.

As I ask much of You,
so You ask much of me.
May I always hear Your call
and respond as a disciple.

I choose Your way.

Let me rest in You,
this day and night.   AMEN

Scripture Readings

Mark 10:17–22   *A choice to make*
Proverbs 3:1–10   *Wise words*

Blessing

In the choosing of God's way,
in the knowing of Christ's love,
in the company of the Spirit,
may I know I am blessed.   AMEN

A Positive Reaction to Jesus' Teaching

'I will give to the poor; and if I have defrauded anyone of anything, I will pay back four times as much.'

~ Luke 19:8 ~

Meditation

Who am I?
To the Romans who have employed me
to do their dirty work, collecting taxes,
I'm just a common Jew
with enough intelligence
to fill in the paperwork, count the coins,
and weedle the last vestiges of wealth from the poorest.

To those I live amongst – grew up amidst,
avoiding me,
because they do not want to be soiled
by my traitorous pattern,
I'm the knock at the door on payday;
I'm the meal they will go without;
the luxury they can't afford.

Within myself I had begun to feel small,
not just in stature,
but encased within the frame of others' views,
unable to remember passion for life
or compassion for the vulnerable.

To the One who passes by,
I am someone to welcome and redeem,
to inspire and gift with hope.
I am taller than my frame,
acknowledged for my possibilities.

Who am I?
I am the unexpected host of grace
that is to be shared.

Morning Prayer

Awaken me this morning,
Rising Son,
opening my eyes to see me as You have made me.
Wonderfully made by You.
May my blemishes bring out the beauty of another,
and my faults inspire me to be generous.
Help me to stand tall in the views that speak of justice
and to clamber through my fears
to meet You in the needs of others.   AMEN

Evening Prayer

Were my conversations high and lofty today?
Did my actions make life more challenging for others?
Lord, call me from the frustrations of this day,
to the space of Your story.
Let the words seep into my heart and thoughts,
so that tomorrow Your grace is gifted
in my activities.   AMEN

Scripture Readings

Luke 19:1–10   *Zacchaeus meets Jesus*
John 4:1–42   *The woman at the well*

Blessing

God of the challenging voice,
help me to hear the pain of the world.
Christ of the pathway,
meet me in the uncertainty of my actions.
Spirit of the hope of difference,
lead me towards those in need of Your love.   AMEN

A Negative Reaction to Jesus' Teaching

'Do you think that I have come to bring peace to the earth? No, I tell you, but rather division!'

~ Luke 12:51 ~

Meditation

A cosy faith, a rosy-eyed view,
and then I open the Book and read Your words.
Astonished, unnerved, You've jarred me again.
I don't want to give up what You tell me to –
I can't sign up to that in this day and age.
You claim too much, always more than I want to give.
I'm offended by Your strong language.
Am I so dark, so evil, so helpless in myself?

'Cut off your hand.'
'Take up your cross.'
'Sell all you have, give to the poor.'
'I AM the resurrection and the life.'
'Whoever believes will be saved, whoever does not will be condemned.'

You mince no words; pull no punches.
Magnetic words.
But shall I be drawn in or pushed away?
The surrounding jury – the people in my life – is out;
some come, some go, when they listen to You.
And what shall I do?
These words of life – can I stomach them?

Morning Prayer

Lord Jesus, I've listened to what You have to say.
I don't like it.
What can I be with You but honest?

I am vulnerable where Your words have pierced me.
Help me trust You and Your command,
living this day in that rawness,
aligning my way with Your words of authority and life.

After all, how else shall I walk?
To whom shall I go?
You have the words of eternal life,
so help me try it Your way.   AMEN

Evening Prayer

Lord Jesus, I come battered and bruised
by a day that was harder because of Your teaching.
Because I lived it. Because I shared it.
Because it's hard to be rejected – You know that.

The more I accept Your will and Your way,
the more I feel the tear away from the world.
Bind up my heart and strengthen my spine.
Help me to sleep and to wake
in uncompromising truth.   AMEN

Scripture Readings

Luke 12:49–53   *A Lord who drives people apart*
John 6:60–69   *Take it or leave it (life or death)*

Blessing

May God the Father enable you
to believe the words of the Son,
to accept the words of the Son,
to live out the words of the Son,
that you may live life to the full
now and forever
in Christ alone.   AMEN

Disabled

*He then said to the paralytic – 'Stand up, take
your bed and go to your home.' And he stood up
and went to his home.*

~ Matthew 9:6–7 ~

Meditation

I had made an enemy of my legs
years ago, when they refused to move.
All I could taste was the dust of others,
walking past me.
Glaring eyes of suspicion
broke me down daily.
I was unforgiven.

Until the day He passed through.
My friends had bundled me to Him,
full of hope – I could see it in their eyes.
This one last chance.
There was no point.
I was unforgiven.

But I could feel the eyes' suspicion,
move from me to Him.
He turned and spoke to me.
I have no idea what He said.
All I knew was that I was standing.

Morning Prayer

As the shards of dawn's light
pierce the darkness,
waking me to the joy of this new day;
as the dust particles dance in the light,
may your Holy Spirit awaken me
to the dance of life itself.
As I stretch and yawn, and wipe sleep from my eyes,
there comes a little more clarity,
a little more colour.

This is the day that You have made for me.
Let me rejoice and be glad in it.
Let the love of Christ shine in my life today.
As I meet new people, may I have the courage
to encounter You, Jesus.   AMEN

Evening Prayer

Jesus,
Sometimes I am afraid of encountering You.
Sometimes I avoid people who are disabled or ill.
Sometimes I cross to the other side.
Sometimes I am blind to the injustice.
Sometimes – if I am really honest –
I ignore the obvious prejudice, uttering words of
discrimination that were once everyday language.
Sometimes I deliberately turn away from those
who are different.

Every time,
every time I do this,
I have missed encountering You, Jesus.
Call me, and I will try and answer.   AMEN

Scripture Readings

Matthew 9:1–8   *The healing of the paralytic man*
Galatians 2:19–21   *New life in Christ*

Blessing

There is too much hardship in this world
not to find joy;
there is too much injustice in this world
not to right the balance;
there is too much pain in this world
not to heal;
every day.

Let us go in peace,
to find grace, healing and wholeness
in all that we do.   AMEN

Young People

But Jesus took him by the hand and lifted him up,
and he was able to stand.

~ Mark 9:27 ~

Meditation

A presence who is silent.
A presence of a young boy
Seriously ill, life disrupted and disabled.
Silent …

A parent who speaks of symptoms:
possession by a spirit and muteness,
a tendency to fall, foam at the mouth, grind teeth,
and become stiff. Turmoil!
A parent who bears the wounds of love.
A parent, the caregiver, who petitions boldly.
Insistent.
'Have pity on us and help us.'
Recognising his own need,
seeking an end to suffering for the family.

Jesus, who said *'Let the children come'*,
listens,
evaluates,
assesses.
Immediately offers the precise care.

Encounter –
taken by the hand,
helped up.
Standing!
Astonishment!
Faith!

Morning Prayer

O Lord, hear me as I pray;
pay attention to my groaning.
Listen to my cry for help, my King and my God,
for I pray to no one but You.
Listen to my voice in the morning, Lord.
Each morning I bring my requests to You and wait
expectantly.

I pray for the voiceless young people:
for those who face illness and disability;
for their families – their advocates and protectors.
Lord, hear their cries, know their needs, be their Helper.
Spread Your protection over them,
that they may be filled with joy;
bless them, O Lord;
surround them with Your shield of love.   AMEN

Evening Prayer

'I believe; help my unbelief!'
For those young people and families
who are drained of hope,
hanging by a few threads, doubting,
help them to hope against hope
that something, even a small thing,
may make for fresh possibilities, astonishment! Faith!
That at the end of each day they may rest amazed,
thankful, filled with appreciation and wonder,
still not knowing quite what to think.   AMEN

Scripture Readings

Mark 9:14–27   *About a boy*
1 Timothy 4:12   *Your youth*

Blessing

May God the Father, Son and Holy Spirit,
who has the power to surprise,
take you by the hand, help you to rise
and enable you to stand in faith.   AMEN

Old People

> *'This is what the Lord has done for me when He
> looked favourably on me and took away the disgrace
> I have endured among my people.'*
>
> ~ Luke 1:25 ~

Meditation

Consider Elizabeth, advanced in years,
bearing a weight of emptiness, troubles and sorrows,
yet persevering in faithfulness.
Unexpected grace explodes!
God's favour comes to her!
Improbable hope now fulfilled.

Consider this holy interruption.
A leaping within her.
Recognition.
Joy.
Impossible hopes now fulfilled.

Righteous.
Rooted in faith.
Shown God's favour,
she flourishes.
God's grace making her fully alive.

In old age life can still be fruitful.
Faith always vital and green,
showing that the Lord is faithful in His care;
not indifferent to sorrow
or to the personal difficulties
we encounter in the course of life.
God's favour comes.

Greet the unexpected, the improbable, the impossible
with joy.
Rejoice in the presence of God.

Morning Prayer

Almighty and wonderful God,
come to us out of Your goodness.
Awaken us to Your favour.
In our emptiness give us Yourself;
for You are enough for us.
Let Your unexpected graces be sufficient.
We can ask for nothing less that can give full honour
to You.
And if we ask anything that is less, we shall be in want,
for only in You have we all that enables us to flourish.
Let Your favour go before me through this day
and all the days of my life.   AMEN

~ Adapted from a prayer of Julian of Norwich ~

Evening Prayer

We rejoice in Your faithfulness that has been shown to us,
for each fresh revelation of Your goodness,
each advent announcing Your good news,
each epiphany of Your presence
in the here and now, to give a future and a hope.

Thank You for surrounding us with Your favour like
a shield.
We rejoice that with the gift of years
life and faith may be transformed and flourish,
bearing fruit for You.
And so we praise You as joy leaps up within this night.
AMEN

Scripture Readings

Luke 1:24–25; 39–45   *Elizabeth's joy*
Psalm 92   *Praise God*

Blessing

Let the favour of the Lord God,
Father, Son and Holy Spirit be upon you
and refresh you with hope.   AMEN

Women

'Have nothing to do with that innocent man,
for today I have suffered a great deal because of
a dream about him.'

~ Matthew 27:19 ~

Meditation

How irrational,
to heed a dream.
How foolish,
to let a disturbed night
cause a distraught day.
How illogical,
to think this could be
speaking truth to power.
How unlikely,
that the judgement will be stopped mid-sentence,
that innocence will be upheld.
How pointless,
this plea to leave the guiltless alone.
How powerless,
the voice of one woman
in a man's world.

But you are remembered,
dream respecter,
advocate of reason,
defender of fair play,
fearless trier,
message sender,
prophetic forewarner,
small-time actor,
unnamed wife,
woman.

Blessed and cursed,
remembered for being ignored.
Woman.

Morning Prayer

Jesus,
before feminism was invented,
You were living outside the lines drawn by men.
In a world entrenched in patriarchy,
You moved outside its dictates.
It is to our shame, Lord,
how far we still have to go to catch up with You.
So judge my thoughts and words today
as a person of my gender among others,
because if You could be good news for all,
so can we.   AMEN

Evening Prayer

Mary's son, Martha's friend,
Susanna's beneficiary, Widow's hero,
give us disturbing dreams that show us Your innocence.
Not guilty of machismo.
Not guilty of assumed superiority.
Not guilty of stereotyping.
Save us, Jesus, for we cannot save ourselves.
Bring to light the disparities to which we remain blind;
the prejudice in which still we live and move;
the comments we unthinkingly pass.
Bring on the day when all are free
to lead, cry, listen, speak, tend, lean and be.   AMEN

Scripture Readings

Matthew 27:11–25   *The conviction of Pilate's wife*
Luke 11:27–28   *A spontaneous affirmation*

Blessing

Blessed be our God,
ungendered,
unhindered,
uncensored.   AMEN

Foreigner

But he had to go through Samaria.

~ John 4:4 ~

Meditation

He could have chosen the longer route,
but for some reason, he didn't;
He chose to go through
a strange land.

They told Him there would be bandits,
robbers, no-gooders
who would strip Him of His clothes,
His possessions,
His pride.
(Or was it theirs that troubled them?)

They told Him that
'nothing good comes out of that place',
that it was
'safer to stick with our own folks'.

The woman He met, though,
was humble, generous and kind.
She gave Him water
from her sacred well.

And they talked.
Of thirst. Of deep wells.
Of living water.
Of springs gushing up to eternal life.

And although her people
and His usually kept
each other at arm's length,
and although their history,
their rituals, their language were different –
there was a shared need for
new life that drew them together
as strangers, no longer, but friends.

Morning Prayer

Lord of the morning,
I rise this day giving thanks
for all that is good and true.
I rise this day seeking openness
to all that is strange or alien to me.   AMEN

Evening Prayer

Lord of the evening,
I take my rest of this day giving thanks
for all that is good and true about the 'other'.
I take my rest of this day
holding in the light any
who are persecuted for their
'otherness'.   AMEN

Scripture Readings

Ephesians 2:11–22   *From stranger to friends*
John 4:1–42   *Jesus meets the woman
from Samaria*

Blessing

May the blessing of Christ Jesus,
once a foreigner in His own land,
be upon us and all we love
this day and always.   AMEN

Roman

'For I also am a man under authority, with soldiers under me; and I say to one, "Go", and he goes.'

~ Matthew 8:9 ~

Meditation

The oppressor's lungs are constricted,
vocal chords hoarse,
heart and limbs heavy,
neck bent with shoulders stooped,
squinting,
a soul held low.
Years spent oppressing empathy,
suppressing doubt,
and impressing power,
have taken their toll,
depressing the soul.
A chain of command
that binds the commander.

Faced with something he is powerless to overcome,
he breaks the links
and runs,
muscles aching,
nerves stinging,
chest tightening.
Admitting he is powerless,
as old lungs inflate
a raspy chuckle,
as weary heart races and limbs pulse,
as head bows,
eyes close,
and soul takes flight.

Morning Prayer

Dear God,
This day, we pray for Your help to break
the cycles of oppression
that trap us in ill-fitting roles,
that hurt the oppressed and the oppressor.
Cast us in better ones.   AMEN

Evening Prayer

Dear God,
we rest and unwind our bodies,
weary,
expectant,
healing,
animated,
pulsing with life.
This night we give ourselves over
to Your care.   AMEN

Scripture Readings

Matthew 8:5–13   *Healing a centurion's servant*
Isaiah 40:12–26   *To whom then will you liken God?*

Blessing

Bless us God,
stretch our vocal chords,
swell our lungs,
jolt our hearts,
and rinse our eyes with tears.
Bless us
as our bodies open and close,
expand and contract,
reach and release,
sustain us in each wind and unwind,
fold and unfold.   AMEN

Moneylenders

If you lend money to my people, to the poor among
you, you shall not deal with them as a creditor;
you shall not exact interest from them.

~ Exodus 22:25 ~

Meditation

You have told us, quite clearly, Lord,
that we can't serve both Mammon and God.
But most of us try.
We seem to want it both ways.

Like the disciples, we don't understand
when You say rich people will find it hard
to enter Your kingdom.

Not that money is bad.
You remind us of all the good it can do,
especially when You are not with us,
and the poor are.

But the love of money will ruin us.

And You were angry with those
who used their powers to line their pockets,
and You drove them out of the temple.

What would You say, dear Lord,
to today's moneylenders?
The bankers and brokers,
the hedgers and betters?
And what to the savers and borrowers,
the spenders and donors?

Tell us again Your good news about money,
so that we do not love it, dear Lord,
but love our neighbour,
and You.

Morning Prayer

Make us Your temples, Lord,
by letting Your Spirit live in us,
and we each become a house of prayer
for all nations.

May we transfer our security
from Mammon to God;
and be neither
borrowers nor lenders,
but receivers and transmitters
of Your grace alone.   AMEN

Evening Prayer

Lord teach me to be wise about money;
to know how to earn it, and spend it,
and save it, and most important of all,
how to give it away;
that our lifestyle might mirror Yours,
proclaiming the riches of the gospel
by sharing the wealth of the nations
and the treasures of heaven
with all people living on earth.   AMEN

Scripture Readings

Exodus 22:25–27   *Do not exact interest*
Mark 10:21–23   *The poor rich man*

Blessing

Bless You Lord for this day, and this night.
What I have received,
I have received from You.
What I have given, is given to You.
May I sleep content,
And live content, now and forever.   AMEN

General Crowd

All Israel heard ... they stood in awe ... because they perceived that the wisdom of God was in him.

~ 1 Kings 3:28 ~

Meditation

What crowd control we find with Solomon,
the man who sorted out two quarrelling women,
in a judgement hall crowded with critical courtiers
enjoying the spectacle.

What crowd control we find with Jesus,
tested by two bickering brothers,
dropping a story into the situation
that would challenge a crowd of spectators,
test them by the judgement of God coming into their midst,
and divide them into threatened worldlings
and awestruck followers.

How do *we* handle crowds, inside the church and outside?

Where do *we* stand in any crowd, when that test turns up:

- with Solomon and Jesus in our judgements?
- with the lovers of God in our responses?
- or fleeing the hot seat as fast as we can?

Morning Prayer

Wise God,
You know the heart of each person in every crowd;
hold me back from quick judgements,
wisecracks, penny lectures, repeated stories;
restrain me from grandstanding,
foolish fantasy and trivial talk;
deliver me from greed unrecognised,
from builder's pride and breaker's yard.

Merciful Christ,
You saw the crowds as sheep without a shepherd;

with Your eyes and Your heart
help me to delight in simple things,
good inheritance, honest praise,
the gifts You give to other people;
grow in me a longing for Your coming
and the sorting out of everything.   AMEN

Evening Prayer

Tonight I reflect upon the issues of today,
for me and for my crowd of fellow creatures:
the conflicts, tough things to decide,
the wars, the hardship of negotiation,
the family feuds, the hidden motives,
all the rotten fruit of prejudice and fear.
Lord have mercy. Christ have mercy. Lord have mercy.

I confess the twist in all our hearts,
the little lusts, the pious propaganda,
our overmuch concern for affirmation.
Lord have mercy. Christ have mercy. Lord have mercy.

I grasp Your hope for me and humankind
that everything will work out for the best.
I pray for love to conquer hate,
for generosity instead of greed,
for peace to replace war,
in short, for kingdom values, kingdom grace.
So grant us peace, grant us Your peace.   AMEN

Scripture Readings

1 Kings 3:16–28   *Solomon dazzles the crowd*
Luke 12:13–21   *The greed of someone in the crowd*

Blessing

From the wonder of God's glorious wealth,
may you be strong in your inner being,
knowing the breadth and length,
the height and depth of Christ's love,
satisfied with the fullness of God.   AMEN

Friends

Some friends play at friendship
but a true friend sticks closer than one's nearest kin.

~ Proverbs 18:24 ~

Meditation

Friend.
The one who
catches the eye of the unseeing,
grabs the attention of the occupied,
captures the interest of the indifferent,
convinces the busy to drop everything.

Friend.
The one who
wines and dines rich and poor as one,
rubs shoulders with the faithful and the doubter,
rewards the loyal and the less than true,
dishes out gifts to the grateful and the grudging.

Friend.
The one who
caresses dirty feet and swallows filthy betrayal,
accepts a tainted kiss and calls it love,
opens his hands to nails and life,
promises paradise to the lost and found.

Friend.
The one who
connects, includes, understands, and loves,
argues, rages, embraces, and loves more,
cries, suffers, reconciles, and loves indiscriminately,
chooses, commissions, commands that we love.

Morning Prayer

If today I find myself
sitting next to the stranger and the strange,
encountering the unclean and the unpopular,
dealing with the dirty and the undesirable,
remind me, Lord, that Your door is an open one,
that Your table has a place for everyone,
that Your hospitality extends to all.
May I be as much of a friend to others
as You are to me.   AMEN

Evening Prayer

Companion Christ,
thank You for Your company today;
for waiting patiently
when I was too busy to speak to You,
for taking a back seat
while I took the lead,
for having my back
when I couldn't see the way forward.

Thank You for your company this night
now that the wee small hours beckon.
May I trust in the company of my Friend
as sleep brings new adventures.   AMEN

Scripture Readings

John 15:12–17   *Love one another*
Proverbs 18:24   *True friendship*

Blessing

Bless the friends who grow with us,
the strangers yet to know us.
Bless us all, God who shows us
the way of love.   AMEN

Disciples

'Make disciples'

Meditation

How does one make a disciple?
What would be the list of ingredients?

An open mind. A faithful heart.
Two ears that listen. Two eyes that see.
Two hands that give. Two feet that walk.
One mouth that speaks good news.

If we have these, are we then disciples?
Discipleship is not limited
to the parts of our body that God has given.
One more thing is necessary:
a willing spirit.

A willing spirit encounters God,
and encounters others.
A willing spirit reaches out in hope,
and dedicates in service.

In our hopefulness and our service,
others encounter our discipleship.
When we commit to justice,
which is what love looks like in public,
then our commitment as Christ's disciples
will be made plain, and others,
inspired, challenged or invited by us,
may choose to follow Him.

Morning Prayer

Lord, this day,
grant me following feet,
that will do justice,
love kindness,
and walk humbly with You.

Lord, this day,
grant me generosity of heart,
that I may share freely
all blessings I have received,
and receive freely,
all blessings others may share with me.

Lord, this day,
make me a better disciple,
following and sharing,
accompanying You,
meeting Your people.
Help me learn and listen.
Help me observe and respond.
Help me practise what You preach.
And all for Your love's sake. AMEN

Evening Prayer

Loving Saviour,
where I have helped another this day
to catch through my imperfect life
a glimpse of Your great light,
I give You thanks.

Eternal Friend,
where I have spoken this day
a word of comfort that has eased
a heavy heart,
I give You thanks.

Wise Teacher,
where I have met this day
other disciples who have opened my mind
to new ways of following You,
I give You thanks.

May I hear this night Your words,
'Well done, good and trustworthy servant',
that I may rest at ease
in Your kindly presence,
and be ready to follow in the coming day
where You will call me.
Through Jesus Christ our Lord.   AMEN

Scripture Readings

Isaiah 52:7–10   *Bringing good news*
Matthew 28:16–20   *Making disciples*

Blessing

Be blessed in your following,
be faithful in your service,
be gentle in your words.   AMEN

PRAYER NOTES

HOW THEY PRAYED

TWELVE ARTICLES ON HOW DEVOTED CHRISTIANS OF THE PAST PRAYED

Rejoice always, pray without ceasing,
give thanks in all circumstances; for this is
the will of God in Christ Jesus for you.

$\sim$ 1 Thessalonians 5:16–18 $\sim$

St Benedict of Nursia
(c.480–c.547)

*Chapter 20. Of Reverence at Prayer: ... how much must
we beseech the Lord God of all things with all humility
and purity of devotion? And let us be assured that it is
not in many words, but in the purity of heart and tears of
compunction that we are heard.*

~ *Rule of St Benedict* ~

St Benedict is perhaps best known for his Rule. He
called it *'a little rule for beginners'*, the purpose being to
assist followers from various backgrounds who entered
his monasteries on their spiritual journey. Rather than
being something rigid and strict, the Rule is intended to
be *'nothing harsh or oppressive'* for them. Benedict's
aim was *'to establish a school of the Lord's service'*
(Prologue 45) in which, confronted with the gospel
demands, the major themes of community, prayer,
hospitality, study, work, humility, stability, peace and
listening all find their expression in the community life.

The Rule provides a framework on which, like the
gymnast, the disciple may exercise. It describes the
pattern of a carefully structured day, a rhythm
incorporating work, study and – significantly – prayer.
Importantly, in all of these things is the requirement
for balance and moderation – that is, not to be consumed
by work, nor to spend so much time in prayer that
responsibilities are neglected. For Benedict, both the
apparatus and the *inner attitude* of prayer are equally
important in aiding disciples in a life of unceasing prayer.

Amidst the busyness and rush of our own lives, we know
that much does consume us, creating an imbalance.
Listening to Benedict, we perceive a balance that comes
from a perspective that views each part of life as
somehow held together and re-orientated around the life
of prayer, such that life is a continuous conversation with
God. This, in turn, anchors prayer in the reality of each

day. There also needs to be balance between solitude and communion with others, silence and conversation.

Through a common liturgy, the routine of prayer and observance of regular liturgical prayer time was, for Benedict, the work of God that connected the community of faith. He provides clear and detailed instructions concerning what is known as the Divine Office – consisting of Morning and Evening Prayer, and in-between the 'Little Hours' and daily Mass, with the day closing with Night Prayer. The rigour of this pattern, which also involved working through all 150 psalms each week, ensured that prayer was marked by regularity and faithfulness, not mood or usefulness.

Benedict was realistic about human nature. He believed that the spiritual life was not some escapism to a quiet life, but something to be worked at. His aim was to build devotional habits of faith that enable service to others, as well as seeking purity of heart to prepare oneself to be in closer union with God.

To that end, for Benedict the book of Psalms is a vital tool in prayer. He understood that the disposition of soul and thought – indeed the whole of life – is somehow encompassed in their words. For Benedict, to listen and attend to the Psalms is to make them in some ways our own, through singing them, reading them out loud, memorising and meditating upon them, whether standing, sitting or kneeling. So exercising, the disciple learns to hold them in their heart throughout each day.

In all these ways, prayer is integrated into every aspect of life and transforms life to one of obedience to Christ's way. Benedict begins the Rule:

> *Listen carefully, ... and incline the ear of your heart (Proverbs 4: 20). Receive willingly and carry out effectively our loving father's advice that by the labour of obedience you may return to Him.*

> ~ Prologue 1,2 ~

Benedict does not expect prayer to be limited to such formal liturgical prayer. He also says that the small chapel should be kept open so that the disciple can go there at any time and pour out the longings of their heart to Christ.

In addition, Benedict says prayers should be short, sharp and from the heart. In other words, informal, passionate prayer is to complement the more formal structured liturgical prayer.

In what ways can Benedict's approach to prayer help inform our own prayer life today? Above all, Benedict provides an adaptable practical wisdom, offering fresh habits in prayer that focus on balance and rhythm in the very ordinary circumstances of workaday life.
For example:

- Consider a combination of fixed prayer times, such as morning and evening, praying the Psalms, and times for freer, more passionate praying.
- Balance this solitude and consider asking others to join in this pattern, agreeing to meet together around prayer and to explore how the key Benedictine themes might be applied and adapted in your lives.
- Further, before a meal or routine task consider *'whenever you begin to do anything say a prayer'* (Prologue 4).

In this way we can begin to weave in practices that provide a framework for regularity and faithfulness towards *unceasing prayer* and become an aid to show respect for the things and people around us.

Undergirding these practical matters there is always to be a reverence at prayer, that expression of commitment to Christ that he calls *'sincere devotion'*, marked by the key virtues of humility and an awareness of the truth of our relationship with God.

Written by FYFE BLAIR

PRAYER NOTES

St Columba
(521–597)

Be a bright flame before me, O God
a guiding star above me.
Be a smooth path below me,
a kindly shepherd behind me
today, tonight, and for ever….

~ Prayer of St Columba ~

There are a variety of prayers attributed to St Columba, the Irish-born abbot who brought Christianity to the shores of Scotland. He established the ancient Iona Abbey, which draws many modern-day pilgrims to both the island, the restored Abbey, and of course the Iona Community. Here many continue to find in his life, works and words an inspiration that is timeless.

Columba's prayers are rooted in *presence* and *place*. From the outset there is an understanding of the presence of God, which is not dependent on the uttering of the prayer, but rather a trust and belief that God is already there. God is in, around and through all things, and the act of prayer does not summon this presence, but recognises its existence.

Rooted in presence, Columba's prayers are also about place. They are about the here and now, and the life of the world around, of which we are always a part. In the example above, it is the images of the natural that are used – of the light a flame casts, the brightness of a shining star, and of the pilgrim path that is travelled. Imagining the power of such light in a dark and brooding landscape, before any form of modern lighting, paints a more dramatic picture of the power of light to illuminate the steps which we faithfully take.

Columba's approach in prayer is both reminiscent of the psalmist, who engaged with the wonder of the natural world around, and of the parables of Jesus, which used organic and agricultural illustrations to speak of truth. From a rootedness in God's presence, in a particular place and point in time, it is the world around that provides the inspiration for Columba's prayer.

Let me bless almighty God,
whose power extends over sea and land,
whose angels watch over all.

Let me study sacred books to calm my soul:
I pray for peace,
kneeling at heaven's gates.

Let me do my daily work,
gathering seaweed, catching fish,
giving food to the poor.

Let me say my daily prayers,
sometimes chanting, sometimes quiet,
always thanking God.

We see in Columba's prayers a simplicity of approach that responds to God's presence and blesses the power of God experienced in nature. There is a grounded understanding of God in the activity of life, and in the purposes of living that life, where nothing is beyond the reach or interest of God.

Often in our approach to prayer we might worry about choosing the right words or expressions, of saying something important enough to address God with, and yet with the prayer of Columba even the seaweed bears mention, along with the necessary activity of fishing to provide food. Poetry in prayer is often created by expressing what is authentic.

How would Columba's prayers translate into our own life of prayer today? Could you find in the supermarket something to praise God for? Could you find in the journey to work a gift to be thankful for? Could you find in the overhead lights of an office space, a metaphor for the light of God in your life? Could you even ask yourself what you might normally hide from God in your prayer life – anger, sadness, hurt?

Columba's prayers invite us to understand that God is eternally present, and call us to pray with the natural words that flow from our lives and the variety of landscapes in which we dwell. There are no boundaries, no rules or no-go areas – God is present, and nothing we can say or do will change the blessing of that truth.

The prayers of Columba affirm a spirituality that allows us to find our home in God wherever we are, physically and mentally, and that may change at times along the way. We are encouraged to have an embodied understanding of our own place in the patterning of our prayers, for we are present to God in the experiences and emotions that we express.

In this encounter and dialogue with God we, with Columba, can trust in God's presence and expect God's love and blessing to be made known.

Alone with none but you, my God
I journey on my way;
what need I fear when you are near,
O Lord of night and day?
More secure am I within your hand
than if a multitude did round me stand.
Amen.

Written by LEZLEY STEWART

PRAYER NOTES

St Hildegard of Bingen
(1098–1179)

The fire has its flame and praises God.
The wind blows the flame and praises God.
In the voice we hear the word which praises God.
And the word, when heard, praises God.
So all of creation is a song of praise to God.

~ St Hildegard of Bingen, *Symphonia Harmoniae*
Celestium Revelationum ~

When St Hildegard of Bingen entered the religious life
(at the age of seven or fourteen, depending on which line
of evidence one accepts), she expected to embark upon a
career dedicated to prayer. Her initial training was to
learn the Psalter by heart along with all the psalm-tones
to which it might be sung, and this formed the basis of
her prayer-life from then until her death. Under the
monastic rule, the offices or 'hours' (sung services in
church) formed the structure of every day, and the meals,
rest and manual work prescribed by the rule were all
subservient to this devotional framework.

Sung prayer was the principal purpose of the monk/nun
in the Middle Ages, praying through song on behalf of
the entire secular world, and St Hildegard built on a
tradition that goes back before Christ to the liturgies of
synagogue and temple. The events of 1178/9, the last year
of her life, reveal the great importance she placed on the
singing of the offices: after a false accusation caused her
community to be placed under an interdict forbidding the
nuns to sing together and denying them access to the
sacraments, she wrote a despairing letter to the
Archbishop of Mainz, pleading that evil would fill the
vacuum created by the lack of corporate sung prayer:

Those who, without just cause, impose silence on a
church and prohibit the singing of God's praises ...
will lose their place among the chorus of angels.

St Hildegard's theology of musical prayer is centred on the concept of the 'cosmic symphony', whereby, at those times when a human community gathers to pray and praise God in sacred music, a temporary connection to heaven is formed, tuned to the nine orders of angels singing eternally around the throne of God. She maintained that the health, both spiritual and physical, of her community depended on this constant communion through song, regulated by the monastic hours. St Hildegard observed no distinction between prayer and praise, viewing them as indivisible, and the war against sin and the Devil was to be won through prayer. She maintained that evil has no music.

For St Hildegard prayer was essentially communal – the very mortar that bound together disparate elements of her community into a strong, mutually supportive, smoothly functioning, and healthy structure. Even when she prayed alone, this was largely a public act: after her death, an eye-witness described how she walked the cloister singing her solo prayers.

Her own collection of 77 sung prayers are works of adoration and devotion, full of wonder and richly painted with devotional imagery. There is no supplication in her texts, by contrast with the human emotions of the Psalter. Her own words and music would have been heard between the psalms and lessons (also sung) so that the two types of spiritual song and each day's diet of Biblical passages commented on each other, sometimes directly and, probably more often, in subliminal ways.

Occasionally, her music was designed as a way of re-affirming faith, vocation and commitment, focusing the mind on a common purpose: a builder of confidence, mutual respect and, even, an appropriately humble form of *esprit de corps*. Her works encourage a visionary, poetic, mystical, even dramatic, opening of the imagination of the community, reaching towards transcendence.

*Through the power of hearing, God opens to human
beings all the glorious sound of the hidden mysteries
and of the choirs of angels by whom God is praised over
and over again.*

*So too, you, O men and women, who are poor and frail
in nature, hear in music ... the sound from the peak of
the living lights shining in the celestial city.*

*Hear the sound from the wonderful words of the
missions of the apostles.*

St Hildegard has much to offer us today. She might
inspire us with her originality, her total lack of repetition,
both in music and text, and her complete avoidance of
the formulaic. From her we might learn how greater
awareness of the words of psalms and hymns, and how
they are arranged in the context of liturgy, increases the
impact and memorability of a service. Does the music
enhance the text or compete with it? Is it enough just to
make any old noise, joyful or otherwise, unto the Lord?
What engages mind, body and spirit together in sung
prayer?

St Hildegard shows us the way that musical prayer can
travel beyond mere sound or, God forbid, entertainment,
to access the numinous.

Written by REBECCA TAVERNER

PRAYER NOTES

St Francis of Assisi
(c.1181–1226)

Most High, all-powerful, good Lord,
Yours are the praises, the glory, and the honour,
and all blessing.
To You alone, Most High, do they belong.

~ St Francis, Opening of *The Canticle of the Creatures* ~

Saint Francis is probably the most popular saint of all. Almost everyone with any kind of Christian background has heard of him and would likely recognise him as a special person who had a particular affinity with all of creation and as a promoter of peace. He is often depicted with the dove of peace in his hand.

Francis saw God in the smallest of creatures, in the birds and bees. He looked at life in all of its natural beauty and marvelled at what God had created. Francis' best-known writing is contained in the *Canticle of the Creatures,* in which he offers the spiritual insight that each aspect of God's creation gives glory and praise to God by being what it was created to be. The sun praises God by giving the world light; the wind praises God by bringing every kind of weather; and the earth praises God by sustaining us through producing fruits, flowers and herbs.

Be praised, my Lord, through all Your creatures,
especially through my lord Brother Sun,
who brings the day; and You give light through him.

Praised be You, my Lord, through Sister Moon
and the stars; in heaven You formed them
clear and precious and beautiful.

~ from *The Canticle of the Creatures* ~

In our own prayer life, do we give time to God, like St Francis, to stop and take note of the wonderful things that surround us? To revel in the glory of the everyday, that becomes so commonplace to us that we may fail even to notice, far less appreciate, the beautiful and extraordinary things in our daily round?

But there is more. It is not just the glorious things that surround us that St Francis comments upon, but the glory of the human person. Here he writes:

Praised be You, My Lord,
through those who give pardon for Your love,
and bear infirmity and tribulation.

Blessed are those who endure in peace, for by You,
Most High, shall they be crowned.

~ from *The Canticle of the Creatures* ~

So, in our prayer life, we are encouraged by St Francis to pause and take time to see God working in and through the creation. Francis wrote to his fellow friars *'all creatures under heaven serve, know, and obey their creator, each according to its own nature, better than you'*. Unlike the sun, wind or water, we can *choose* to live in accord with our truest selves, or not; to praise God by our words and deeds, or not; to recognise our place in the family of creation, or pretend that we are the master of it.

But there is an important addition. St Francis is not praising God's creation for its own sake, or simply because God created everything. There is a deeper meaning that should inform our daily prayer.

One of the most famous prayers attributed to St Francis is the 'Prayer of St Francis', although it is believed to be only around 100 years old. Nevertheless, the Franciscan Order recommends it as a *'simple prayer for peace'*, and there is a fundamental truth in the prayer that reflects the deepest longings of St Francis. It is a call and a prayer to hold all things in balance. So often we see lives, perhaps our own, 'out of kilter' and feel overwhelmed by events or surroundings. Francis calls us to return to a place and a state that brings balance. So, the prayer is to be understood when we are misunderstood, to offer love instead of hate, to be forgiven when we have brought hurt and disorder to others and the created order. These are qualities Our Lord Jesus Christ prayed for, and St Francis sought to live out that balance, to be that example.

Lord, make me an instrument of your peace;
where there is hatred, let me sow love;
where there is injury, pardon;
where there is doubt, faith;
where there is despair, hope;
where there is darkness, light;
where there is sadness, joy.

O Divine Master, grant that I may not so much seek
to be consoled as to console;
to be understood as to understand;
to be loved as to love.

For it is in giving that we receive;
it is in pardoning that we are pardoned;
and it is in dying that we are born to eternal life.

~ Prayer of St Francis ~

St Francis offers an exemplar of a life held in balance through prayer, of the need to hold humanity and all of creation in harmony. The model of his life is a call to pray that we may become authentic human beings where there is no distinction between a life lived and a prayer prayed. On that path lies true peace.

Written by BOB FYFFE

PRAYER NOTES

Julian of Norwich
(1342–c.1416)

Pray wholeheartedly, though you may feel nothing, though you may see nothing, yes, though you think that you could not, for in dryness and barrenness, in sickness and in weakness, then is your prayer most pleasing to me.

~ Julian of Norwich, *Revelations of Divine Love* ~

Julian of Norwich was a medieval lay Christian who spent at least part of her life living as a recluse in the city of Norwich. She was exceptional in her own day: first, she was a woman (who may well have been married and widowed) and a theologian; second, at a time when almost all spiritual writing was based either on Scripture or on an academic theological problem, her writing was based directly on her own experience of a life-threatening illness and of how God became real to her in and through it.

She is like a latter-day psalmist, refusing to give up on God even in the midst of terrible suffering, refusing to accept that such suffering is either meaningless or to be piously accepted. Instead, she digs deep down into what has happened to her in search of a God who can help her make sense of it. Like the psalmist, she does not hesitate to quote God's actual words to her – as in the quotation above. This is not out of some fanciful sentimentalism, but is a result of a lengthy period of contemplative reflection on what has happened to her. Out of this emerges a faith at once defiant and submissive: defiant of limp religious platitudes; submissive to the God whose own suffering in the person and death of Jesus at last enables her to make sense of her own.

Julian begins not with her own sufferings but with those of Christ, whose costly, unconditional love for us is, for Julian, that of a mother for her children. Devotion to the

Passion of Christ was widespread in the later Middle Ages, in part a response to traumatic events such as the Black Death and the Hundred Years War. But Julian's devotion goes far beyond mere feelings; although her prayer (again like that of the Psalms) gives much space for the honest articulation of feelings, it refuses to separate them from hard-edged intellectual questioning. As in the words quoted at the start, her strong belief is that God is telling her to persist in prayer irrespective of how she feels.

More importantly, *'prayer unites the soul to God'* through the identification of our suffering with that of Christ. Prayer is precisely the action of those who do not see God, in order that they might do so:

> *When we see nothing of God, then we need to pray to Jesus because we are failing, and in order to strengthen ourselves.*

And because prayer unites us with God, it is effective, since from all eternity God has willed certain things to happen through our prayer. As Denys Turner puts it in his book, *Julian of Norwich, Theologian:*

> *Prayer is not how we get God to do things for us. Prayer is how God gets things done by means of us.*

There is one other, crucial, sense in which Julian's prayer resembles that of the psalmist. Despite her life as a recluse, and her prolonged experience of serious illness, there is nothing remotely private or introspective about either Julian's faith or her prayer. For Julian, the 'I' is always inseparable from the 'we':

> *For I am sure there are very many that never had revelations or visions, but only the common teaching of Holy Church, who love God better than I. If I pay special attention to myself, I am nothing at all; but in all things I am in the unity of love with all my fellow-Christians.*

Hence:

> *the more that I love in this way whilst I am here, the more I am like the joy that I shall have in heaven without end.*

These are words that apply as much today in the 21st century as they did when Julian wrote them.

Like the psalmist, Julian encourages us to be bold in bringing our deepest longings and our most difficult questions into our prayer, because both the psalmist and Julian came to believe that they were unconditionally loved – the psalmist through God's unique covenant with Israel, Julian through her acute perception of the maternal love of God we experience supremely in Jesus' suffering on the cross.

Julian's prayer is extraordinarily visual, contemplative in the literal sense of the word. She wants us to look unblinkingly at the cross, and then to hold up against it the suffering of the world – and our own suffering too. Then she wants us to let the love that seeps through the wood and the nails (this is the kind of language she uses) flood over and into our pain, and that of all the world, so that the love revealed on the cross soaks into and embraces the sorrows of creation. And that is what prayer is all about.

> *So I was taught that love is our Lord's meaning.*
> *And I saw very certainly in this and in everything,*
> *that before God made us he loved us, which love was*
> *never shaken, and never shall be.*

Written by GORDON MURSELL

PRAYER NOTES

St Ignatius of Loyola
(1491–1556)

The unexamined life is not worth living.

~ Socrates ~

'In a busy life if you follow only one kind of prayer, let it be the Examen', so said Ignatius of Loyola in his own 16th-century vernacular to his Jesuit novices. The Examen? This is a way of reflecting on or reviewing the day so as to notice the inner movements in our soul – movements *towards* God or *away* from God, thereby becoming more aware of our responses to life, and to God's presence, and making good choices for our lives.

Ignatius began his own spiritual quest following a literally shattering encounter with a cannonball. Initially, during many months of recuperation, he noticed the difference in his mood after reading stories of, and daydreaming about, chivalrous deeds of soldiers and knights; these lifted him for a while, but then left him in gloom and despondency. However, when he read the lives of the saints, and of Christ, and imagined himself doing likewise, his heart lifted and stayed this way, full of spiritual consolation. This noticing of where his attention had been as his mood ebbed and flowed became the basis of 'Ignatian discernment'. Although Ignatius was also well known for his use of 'imaginative contemplation', the Examen was his first call to prayer for busy people wanting to notice where God is to be found – and this can reach through to our hectic 21st-century lives too, as outlined in the next few paragraphs.

One of the few rules that Ignatius made for the Jesuit order was to practise the Examen twice daily, at noon and at the end of the day. We might start once a day, for 10 or 15 minutes looking back on the day, recalling encounters and events, noticing thoughts, feelings, reactions and responses to help us become more aware of where God's love and grace has been present to us. This will help us become attuned to the sacred in the everyday – and also help us to perceive where we might have missed those 'God moments' and could choose differently the next day.

- Begin by **stilling yourself**, asking that only love will guide your reflections, so you can see the day through God's eyes of unconditional love, the most accepting, compassionate, kind eyes you could imagine.

- As you look back, ask for **grace to resist the temptation to judge yourself**, but rather simply to notice what stirs in your awareness, with the desire for more intimate knowledge of self and God – and for the transformation that comes from the deepening relationship between the two. We tenderly 'examine' our lives in order to participate with and learn from God, not to judge.

- Then slowly **let your mind and heart wander back** over the events of the day – not necessarily in every detail, but seeing what stands out for you, what is still 'alive' in you with feeling. Just notice; don't rush or grab to pinpoint a memory.

- Perhaps something gave you a particular sense of **being alive**, a specialness, surprise or encouragement? Was there a moment that 'flowed'? When were you able to give love, or feel in harmony with God's love for our world?

- Take time to **savour and give thanks**, and to notice where this movement arose from and any insight it brings. Looking back, how did God seem to you at this time in your day?

- Think too about any **difficult or painful** thoughts, feelings or encounters today: maybe an argument or criticism; a worry or unease. Was there something around which made you feel resentful, drained or stuck? What was happening in your relationship with yourself at this time? And around your sense of God?

Where might you have gone your own way, and lost sight of God's kingdom values?

● **Talk with God** about what you remember and how you feel, and wait in openness. What might God be showing you through the ups and downs of the day? And with any new **insights**, take a moment to ask for help to express – and receive – God's love more fully tomorrow.

Ignatius was a brilliant psychologist – long before the concept was coined – and today we might see many overlaps between the Examen and the psychological field, such as the focus in cognitive behavioural therapy on the interaction between thought and mood, or psychotherapy's exploration of unconscious process and desire, or the goals of mindfulness, which brings awareness to 'the moment' without judgement.

In the Examen comes the soul's deepest cries, a prayer of honesty where all can be laid bare before the God of love, transformed through greater compassion and awareness, and offering a way to make choices for the greatest life. What are you most grateful for today? What are you least grateful for today? In your 'review of the day', start there.

Written by ELIZABETH WHITE

Elizabeth White is a spiritual director, trainer and pastoral supervisor.
www.reflectivespaces.org.uk

Further Resources:

www.pray-as-you-go.org daily meditations which include an audio version of the Examen

Sleeping with Bread by the Linns; an accessible, compact introduction to the Examen

Making Heart Bread also by the Linns; a beautiful children's book teaching 'the prayer of review'

PRAYER NOTES

John Knox
(c.1513–1572)

Anyone wanting to pray must know and understand
that prayer is an earnest and familiar talking with
God, to whom we declare our miseries, whose support
and help we implore and desire in our adversities,
and whom we laud and praise for our benefits received
... as the psalms of David do clearly teach.

~ John Knox,
Confession and Declaration of Prayers (1554) ~

John Knox grounded his concept of prayer in Scripture, theology, history and human reality. It does not relate to some separate sphere of benign and cosy 'spirituality', taking the soul for a private, relaxing and free-ranging walk in order to induce a sense of personal wellbeing encouraged by the prospect of tangible benefit. To Knox, 'perfect' Christian prayer is not an option; it is divinely commanded and may even use fasting (as in the Bible) to help intensify spiritual awareness.

For Knox, there are shadows of fear and judgement. There is, however, reassurance and certainty that, through the mediating intercession of Jesus Christ and with the inspirational aid of the Spirit, God gladly entertains the unburdening and supplications of those with faith in His promises. These promises are mercy and forgiveness of, for example, improper worship and attitudes or behaviour damaging to self and others. Insisting that Christ is the appointed messenger of messages to and from God in the context of 'talking' with Him, Knox in the *Declaration* quotes Ambrose of Milan: '*[Christ] alone is our mouth, through which we speak to God. He is our eye, through which we see God. He is our right hand, by whom we offer anything to the Father. Unless He intercedes, there is no interaction with God for us or all the saints.*'

Prayer, then, is a 'conversation with God' in which we can only properly engage if we first acknowledge our conceited self-sufficiency and complacency. The Biblical model for this is found especially in the Psalms. Before Knox, the dialogue idea was emphasised by Early Church Fathers such as Augustine (also quoted by Knox), Gregory of Nyssa, Ambrose of Milan, John Cassian, Benedict of Nursia, and especially by Reformers such as Luther ('God calls us first') and Calvin ('prayer is a mutual, if unequal, discourse with God'). Therefore, proper prayer is a two-way process, not a one-way transmission of praise and requests to a distant deity. For Knox, prayer is an unveiling – *'hard and difficult'* – of the impaired self, whether individual or corporate, a confession seeking remedy from *'the Physician'*.

Divine answers to prayers may well be, Knox suggested, *'deferred'*, especially if God is momentarily *'crabbit'* (a better word of Knox's rather than our 'wrath' or 'anger'). Patience and perseverance, twins of faith and hope, are the badges of the Christian character. If God often keeps us waiting ('tarrying'), as it were, the reason is for *'the exercise and trial of our faith, and not that He sleeps or is absent from us at any time (Ps. 44:23–4; 121:4), but that with more gladness we might receive that which ... we have awaited ... assured of His eternal providence' (Declaration)*

Even so, Knox was distressed about the general lack of renewal in Christian living. In later life, he suffered depressions and religious disillusionment because of his perception of God's self-restraint in the face of disorder and impiety in society – other than occasioning earthly miseries as reminders. Yet Knox refused to blame God for not ushering in effective transformation, rather blaming himself and fellow-believers as well as the majority with fake faith. He believed that this followed from insufficient remorse for infringing the Ten Commandments and from a lack of determination to change their ways.

As with his sermons, few Knox prayers have survived. Following an old misconception that the original *Book of Common Order* (1562) was 'Knox's Liturgy', its prayers were seen as his, whereas it was a collective composition. Some appended prayers do, however, seem to be Knox's, such as 'A Godlie Prayer', reproduced in Alec Cheyne's *Scottish Piety*. One formulation encapsulates the gospel heart: *'Seeing our debt is great, which you have forgiven us in Jesus Christ, make us love you and our neighbours all the more.'*

Other Knox prayer material is in Henry Sefton's *John Knox*, part of The Devotional Library series. The self-flagellating Knox is exemplified in 'A Prayer in Time of Trouble': *'In youth, mid-age, and now after many battles, I find nothing in me but vanity and corruption.'* Knox's *Declaration* ended with a 'Confession', in which he pleads: *'Let us not faint under the cross of the Saviour,'* that is, enable Christianity to withstand the abuse of its despisers.

Knox reminds us that 'praying to God' is not simply us speaking and God listening passively. Furthermore, as members of Christ's body, our prayers should be directed to Jesus Christ aided by the Holy Spirit, so that we may detect more easily the voice of God in inner conversation. Knox admits that true prayer is tough: we need to shed self-admiration, to declare our disguised weakness and to recognise that *'our help'* comes from beyond, not from within. But the greatest obstacle is creeping unbelief:

> *I know the complaints ... the anger that [human nature] has against God, calling all his promises in doubt and being ready every hour to lapse from God – against which remains only faith and ... the assistance of God's Spirit.*

Written by Ian Hazlett

Note: The original Scots-English text of the *Declaration* is in Laing's *Works of John Knox*, vol. 3. A modernised English version is available online and in book form provided by an American 'Presbyterian Heritage' enterprise. To give a word of caution: the *Declaration* is mostly a translation from Book III, chap. 20 of Calvin's *Institutes*, and follows the pattern of Calvin's 'Four Rules' for prayer bound to Christ's intercession. This means that on prayer, Knox and Calvin are speaking with one voice.

PRAYER NOTES

St Teresa of Ávila
(1515–1582)

*Considering your strict enclosure, the little recreation
you have, my sisters, and how many conveniences are
wanting in some of your convents, I think it may console
you to enjoy yourselves in this Interior Castle, where you
can enter, and walk about at will, at any hour you please,
without asking leave of your superiors.*

~ Teresa of Ávila ~

Teresa, who died in her home country of Spain at the age
of 67, was a Carmelite nun who wrote prolifically on
prayer from a context of illness, spiritual distress and
Godly visions. In founding Discalced ('without shoes')
Carmelite houses, in the way of Ignatius of Loyola,
Teresa put into practice her evident leadership skills and
her deep desire to live as close to a hermetic life as
possible. Teresa's writings include the *The Way of
Perfection*, a contemplative commentary on the Lord's
Prayer. She also wrote *The Book of the Foundations* for
her nun-companions, and recorded her autobiography in
her *Life*.

Her autobiography explores the life of prayer through the
image of *'four waters'*, likening prayer to four ways of
watering with a progressive lessening of human effort.
The first *'watering'* is as if from a well: first we must
find the well of prayer, then we must find a vessel with
which to draw the water that will nourish our soul.
The second way of being drenched in prayer is through a
water-wheel: water flows in the stream, but we must
catch it, harness it, in order to quench our thirst.
Third, prayer is like the stream itself: we enter and are
encompassed in prayer. Then, finally, the only human
effort needed is to stand still, to be soaked by the rain:
the fourth image of prayer as water.

This sense of deepening, of prayer requiring progressively less human input, and increasingly more stillness and awareness of the encompassing nature of God's love, is taken up and developed in what is Teresa's most powerful work on prayer: *The Interior Castle*.

Written over four weeks, initially for the sisters in her religious community for whom an *'interior castle'* took the place of external trappings, Teresa was often found *'in a state of reverence and intensity'* by those who lived in close community with her. These periods of intense spiritual revery were accompanied by times of illness. Teresa here imagines *'the soul as resembling a castle, formed of a single diamond or a very transparent crystal'*, where the pilgrim progresses from the outer courtyard to its centre, peeling back layers of identity and experience until a union with God, devoid of clutter, is found.

Inside the castle are seven *'mansions'*, or *'dwelling places'*, each one taking us closer to union with God who is waiting for us at the centre. Our journey through the gate into this castle is assumed to be a journey rooted in prayer and meditation.

Moving through the first three mansions, described as the *'purgative way'*, the pilgrim encounters demons, suffering, setbacks and temptations to remain in these outer mansions, *'lacking determination to quit their present condition'*. Teresa encourages the reader to continue on the journey, deepening our life of prayer as we move closer to the *'kernel'* at the heart of the crystal, and to resist the temptation to settle for a mediocre prayer life. Much of the journey through these first mansions is a journey of self-discovery.

Like peeling away the layers of an onion, Teresa's journey takes us next to the fourth mansion, where *'prayer of recollection'* is an invitation to reflect on the life lived so far. This and the final three mansions take the pilgrim to a deeper level of contemplation or mystical prayer. Increasingly, as the soul gives itself over to God in humility through daily prayer and meditation, human distraction and material temptations are left behind.

The final three mansions are experiences of union with God in increasing measure, with parallels to the four ways of watering described earlier. Each stage in our deepening union with God relies on increasingly less human dependence, and on greater unity with God. The fifth mansion is a place of preparation for this union as in a promise or a betrothal; the sixth mansion is a union as of lovers; the seventh is a union, or marriage with God where the soul achieves clarity.

In all of this, Teresa affirms her inseparability from her love for Christ and the Church, including participation in the sacraments. She stresses her own lack of insight and wisdom, attributing her works to the voice of God speaking in and through her.

The mystical intensity of Teresa's prayer life may seem far removed from everyday life in 21st-century Scotland, but there are many pertinent questions, or gifts, that we can take from Teresa's writings:

- To what extent is your prayer life connected to times of prolonged mystical meditation? Or could it be?
- What is your response in your prayer life when you find yourself in the *second mansion*, feeling trapped or *lacking determination to quit your present condition*?
- What experiences of prayer have taken you close to union with God? How can you intensify those?

Written by RUTH HARVEY

PRAYER NOTES

James Melville
(1556–1614)

Pray continually, says the Spirite of God be his Apostle.
And not without cause: for it is the maist Godly,
charitable, profitable, comfortable, honourable,
and sa the best exercise of aluther [everything] ...

~ James Melville, from 'Ane Short Exhortation to prayer
prefixed' from *A Spirituall Propine of a Pastour to his People*
(Edinburgh, Robert Waldegrave, 1589) ~

Raised at Baldovie near Montrose, James Melville was
the son of one of the first generation of Reformed
ministers after 1560. As a young man he was taken under
the wing of his uncle Andrew, a rising star of European
theology who was later to become a highly polarising
figure in the struggles over the polity of the Church and
the role of the monarch within it. James was a very
different and more pastoral figure, and in 1586 he gave
up academia for parish ministry in the East Neuk of Fife.

James Melville's outlook on life is clear to see in the
pages of his extensive *Autobiography and Diary*, which
reflects on all kinds of personal struggles as well as the
great affairs of Church and State. However, of even
greater value from the point of view of his approach to
prayer and spirituality is his 1589 publication *A Spirituall
Propine [gift] of a Pastour to his People*. It is dedicated
to *'The Reverende Fathers and Brethren, Elders of the
Congregation of Kilrinny, and hail [whole] flocke
committed to their governement'*.

Melville reflected the widespread belief that singing was
an important element of prayer. In those days, singing in
church was focused upon the 'smash hits' of the day, the
Psalms of David in metre, sung to a wide range of tunes
appropriate to the different moods of the texts. He built
on this phenomenon in his new spiritual manual by
writing religious poetry which could be sung to the well-
known tunes of the Psalter. His firm conviction was that

poetry and singing would *'delyte the mind'*, *'move sa the affections'*, and *'stirre up and set the force of the soules affections towards God, in pleasand meditation thereof'*. Music was not a decoration, but a mode of prayer.

The foundation of prayer was Scripture, and Melville urged his people to *'heare, reade, studie, and meditate the word of God'*. It is important to remember that Scripture was memorised and internalised then in a way that is less common in our world of sensory and information overload. The effect of this was that the language of prayer was soaked in familiarity with Scripture and psalmody, drawn up from the depths of one's being.

Prayer was to begin with yourself, extend to family devotions, and then to public worship. Melville encouraged his people to be *'hamely [homely] with God'* and to bring all of the details of their lives before God in a very intimate way, being open to the work of the Holy Spirit. For Melville and his contemporaries, there was a highly emotive connection with God in prayer, which was urged at morning, noon and night, not only in private but in the workplace, where he encouraged prayer *'with songs, as with salt to season the actiones'*. One can imagine that in a Scotland where Christianity was the norm, such a public devotional life was not as unusual as it might now sound!

In addition to poetry, *A Spirituall Propine* contained a large number of composed prayers that could be used at various different times and seasons. It is interesting that the leading figures of the early Reformed Kirk were quite relaxed about the composition and use of such prayers. They could be used as they were set, but they were also designed to help people to develop their own praying voice. A measure of success for Melville would have been to know that his congregation were able to make their own devotions without having to rely continually on his primer.

James Melville's primary motivation in urging his people to prayer was that they would be in right relationship with God, saying that *'the dayly wish of my heart is for the effectual working of the quickening spirit of Christ in all your hearts'*. If that relationship was right, their future in the life to come would be assured. His was a fundamentally pastoral concern for his congregation's spiritual wellbeing.

James Melville's work speaks very freshly into an environment where, in a sense, we are continually re-learning the language of prayer. He was an innovator who appreciated the issues of attention span and motivation, which are still a challenge for us. He found a remedy for his time in the use of poetic imagery and popular music to carry and inspire prayer and connection with God. All of this seems to be an encouragement to us to explore fresh expressions of prayer rooted in Scripture and to be confident that prayer is always to be our unique and intimate conversation with God.

> *Grant, Lord, that we may be strengthened by the Spirit*
> *in the inward man, that thy Christ may dwell in our*
> *hearts by faith; that we being rooted and grounded*
> *in love, may be able to comprehend with all the saints;*
> *what is the breadth and length, the depth and height of*
> *that inestimable grace, redemption, and glorie, that*
> *thou hast prepared for them, and to embrace that love*
> *of Christ, whilk [which] passeth all understanding,*
> *that wee may be filled with all fulnesse of God.*

From 'A maist pithie prayer, for obteining of the working of the Halie Spirit, by the word and sacraments' in *A Spirituall Propine*

Written by MARTIN RITCHIE

NB: Original spellings in the above quotations (with Scots orthography of the period) have been retained from the 1589 edition.

PRAYER NOTES

John Wesley
(1703–1791)

The chief means of grace are prayer, whether in secret or with the great congregation; reading, hearing, and meditating on the Scriptures ... and receiving the Lord's Supper ... and these we believe to be ordained of God, as the ordinary channels of conveying his grace ...

~ Extract from John Wesley's Sermon,
'The Means of Grace' (1746) ~

In a Lincolnshire rectory, mostly under the direction of their learned and gifted mother, the infant Wesleys were reared on a daily prayer routine. Susanna Wesley recorded:

Our children were taught, as soon as they could speak, the Lord's Prayer to which as they grew older, were added prayers for their parents, some collects and portions of scripture, as their memories could bear. They were to be still at family prayers before they could kneel or speak.

John Wesley's devotional life was saturated with the Book of Common Prayer. This he described as *'the finest liturgy in the world'*. A daily round of praise, confession, thanksgiving and intercession was offered in the time-honoured language of Morning and Evening Prayer. Day by day, Wesley recited the appointed psalms, later in life editing out, for others, the parts he thought *'unfit for the ears of a Christian congregation'*!

Wesley's first publication, in 1733, was *A Collection of Forms of Prayer for Every Day in the Week*. As was the custom of his age, Wesley borrowed mercilessly from the prayers of earlier spiritual guides such as Thomas Ken.

Being created by thee, let me live to thee;
being created for thee, let me ever act for thy glory;
being redeemed by thee, let me render unto thee what is thine, and let my spirit ever cleave to thee alone.

Extempore or free prayer was a vital aspect of Methodist spirituality. One of Wesley's preachers testified, *'Such a prayer as Mr. Wesley's I have never heard in my life'*. At the close of his abridgement of the Communion Office, Wesley suggested *'Then the [minister], if he see it expedient, may put up a prayer extempore'*.

Such 'conceived prayer', or 'prayer from the heart', although extemporised, retained a doctrinal orthodoxy governed by the imbibed language and phrases of the Bible, the Prayer Book and Methodist hymnody. What came out was blessed by what had gone in! Wesley studiously avoided such 'economic' phrases as 'Creator, Redeemer and Sanctifier' in addressing the Trinity: *'the quaint device of styling them three offices rather than persons gives up the whole doctrine'*.

From the English Puritan tradition Wesley inherited the custom of calling his people to the annual renewal of their Christian vows and promises, in the searching words of his Covenant Service.

Lord, Jesus ... I put myself wholly into thy hands:
put me to what thou wilt, rank me with whom thou wilt;
put me to doing, put me to suffering,
let me be employed for thee or laid aside for thee ...

let me be full, let me be empty,
let me have all things, let me have nothing,
I freely and heartily resign all to thy pleasure and
disposal.

Father, Son and Holy Ghost ...
thou art now become my Covenant-Friend,
and I ... am become thy Covenant-Servant.
And the Covenant which I have made on earth,
let it be ratified in heaven.

~ *Directions for Renewing our Covenant with God*, 1780 ~

(For a contemporary version based on Wesley's 'Covenant Service', see *Common Order*, 1994, pages 343–7.)

Wesley's 50-year ministry, a punishing schedule of preaching, publishing and organising, was wholly dependent on his daily prayer discipline. *'I have so much to do that I spend several hours in prayer before I am able to do it'.* The small 'prayer room' still to be seen in Wesley's London house has often been described as 'the power-house of Methodism'.

> *Here then far from the busy ways ... I sit down alone; only God is here. In His presence I open, I read His book; for this end, to find the way to heaven. I lift up my heart to the Father of Lights.*
>
> ~ Preface to *Sermons on Several Occasions*, 1747 ~

John, together with his younger brother, Charles, who wrote about 2,500 hymns, taught the early Methodists that *'poetry was the handmaid of piety'*. In the words of present-day Methodist, Colin Morris, *'a good hymn is a theological time-bomb planted in the mind – you never know when it is going to go off'*. John himself made some abiding translations of Lutheran and Moravian hymns.

What gifts for our own prayer life has Wesley handed on to us? These gifts are many:

- Foremost, a serious daily appointment with God, with properly allocated time, in a designated place.
- A prayer time enriched by the written devotions of our forbears and contemporaries.
- Crucially, preparing for and attending Holy Communion and an annual covenanted commitment to Christian discipleship.
- Vitally, both alone and in groups, the use of extempore or direct prayer furnished by Christian reading and guided by the Spirit.
- Constantly allowing the theology of our prayers to be informed and enriched from the hymnbook and Psalter.

Written by NORMAN WALLWORK

PRAYER NOTES

Thomas Merton
(1915–1968)

Yet there is that all-important stillness, and listening to God, which seems to be inertia, and yet is the highest action.

~ Thomas Merton ~

Thomas Merton prayed with and, more often, without words. After studying at Columbia University in New York, he dedicated the rest of his life to the practice of contemplative prayer as a Trappist monk in Gethsemane Monastery, Kentucky. His prayers with words were simple and honest in the way of the Desert Fathers. His prayers without words were about coming into the presence of God with nothing at all – not even words – and surrendering his heart and mind to the silence.

Contemplative prayer

Contemplative prayer for Merton was about drawing to stillness in silence to find *'one's deepest center, awaking the profound depths of our being in the presence of God who is the source of our being and our life'.*

It is in this place of silence that all that is otherwise avoided by keeping busy or drowned out in the humdrum of life is now faced up to and can be addressed. What is false and pretentious is exposed, and the real and true self is discovered.

Merton cautioned against narcissistic introspection in contemplative prayer; rather he encouraged those praying to see themselves in the light of God, to realise that the very desire to pray is itself inspired by God.

It is the movement of trust, of gratitude, of adoration, or of sorrow that places us before God, seeing both Him and ourselves in the light of His infinite truth.

Merton understood this way of prayer not as trying to find God in silence but rather a time to rest in the one already found *'who loves us, who is near to us, who comes to draw us to himself'.*

He regarded the silence itself as an act of worship, orientating towards God regardless of the mood of the one praying. Viewing the silence as an act of worship was the most important thing, more important than any attempt to hear God saying anything.

Merton was not oblivious to the distractions that often crowd in when trying to be silent and still before God. He advised that when it is not possible to avoid distractions, these thoughts could be turned into the theme and motivation of the prayers.

He encouraged the one praying to take every thought captive to God. But he aspired – and inspired others – to achieve the state of prayer where the one praying is no longer self-conscious. Merton described the purest form of prayer as something on which it is *'impossible to reflect until after it is over'.*

The journey to this experience of prayer was a lifelong pursuit of Merton's, leading him to live in solitude in a hermitage away from the rest of the monastic community. It also led him to learn the practices of contemplation and meditation from other faiths, ultimately leading him to Asia, where he died in December 1968.

Prayerful action

For Merton, this form of prayer in stillness, silence and solitude was itself an action and also a precursor to fruitful action in the world. Even though he chose to live in a monastic community, and later in solitude, Merton was often very publicly outspoken on issues of peace and justice. For Merton, there was a close relationship between contemplation and action. He understood that in coming to a place of stillness and silence before God, we can sense the presence of the divine and, drawing from that presence, we are moved to recognise God's presence in others and the surrounding world.

Merton emphasised that prayer without action was not communion with the God who is love, and action without the *'deep apprehension of the ground and source of love was inevitably futile and frustrating'*

It was in the monastery that Merton assumed responsibility for the world rather than retreating away from it, his solitude and contemplation giving him a perspective few others had. This perspective was initiated in a dramatic moment in his life when he had an epiphany of love for humanity as he stood at the corner of 4th and Walnut Street in Louisville. He wrote in his journal later:

I am still a member of the human race, and what more glorious destiny is there for man, since the Word was made flesh and became, too, a member of the Human Race!

In the turbulent political and environmental times of today, Merton's contemplative prayer offers us guidance and a means of prayerful resistance in the world. It also cautions us that:

Without contemplation, without the intimate, silent, secret pursuit of truth through love, our action loses itself in the world and becomes dangerous.

Written by WENDY YOUNG

PRAYER NOTES

Mother Teresa
(1910–1997)

We ourselves feel that what we are doing is just a drop in the ocean. But the ocean would be less because of that missing drop.

~ Mother Teresa ~

There is a story of a conversation Mother Teresa had with an inquirer when asked about her prayer life. The inquirer apparently asked as perhaps we would all have done if we had had the same opportunity, *'When you pray, what do you say to God?'*

Mother Teresa's reply was quite simple and stark: *'I don't talk. I only listen.'*

The inquirer didn't want the conversation to end so briefly and after a moment's pause asked, *'Then what is it God says to you?'*

Mother Teresa smiled, looked to the ground and said, *'God doesn't talk either. God also listens.'*

The inquirer was confused and hesitated, trying to form the next question but, unsure of what to ask, Mother Teresa helped fill the silence, *'I'm sorry you don't understand what I mean, but really there is no other way I can explain it.'*

For Mother Teresa, prayer seemed to be a place of encounter, or living within the presence of God. Her experience was that prayer is less conversation and more 'being with' and 'being in' the company of love and grace. And it is enough.

From such a way of being comes the possibility of the journey towards each other, our neighbour, without the lines of authority, power or status. It starts with listening and ends with that person beside us, together with their need and our own need, as we engage with each other's being. It begins, not with instructions and wants, but with love, and ends in the acts of love we offer to our neighbour and that our neighbour offers us.

And we could leave it there. That is indeed enough. Mother Teresa, however, didn't always find it as simple as that. Over the course of 50 years, she wrote almost 40 letters to her spiritual directors that showed that, despite what we might presume of her confidence in God and certainty in faith, she suffered what St John of the Cross described as *'a dark night of the soul'*, where she felt a total abandonment by God in her prayers.

> *In my soul I feel just that terrible pain of loss, of God not wanting me – of God not being God – of God not existing.*

These are words she wrote in 1959 and these feelings never left her for the next five decades. Mother Teresa, however, would not describe such feelings as a loss of belief; over time and with the help of her spiritual directors, she came to recognise this 'dark night' as a way of experiencing what so many feel in the world, especially those whom she and her order accompanied through life and death. Indeed, such feelings in herself came very soon after she began working with those who many said had no hope.

Saint John of the Cross never explained the 'dark night of the soul' as being deserted by God, but rather as a way of *love* whereby feelings of loss were a means to help cut ties with earthly things. It must have been a hard and perhaps frightening experience for Mother Teresa when she could find *'no words to express the depths of darkness'*.

Surely this is also the experience at times of many of us? Does it make it easier to know that some of those we imagine to be closest to God felt the same way?

Mother Teresa's response to this didn't come immediately but only over time. She concluded, through the help of her spiritual directors, that through her experience of abandonment she could identify with the abandonment Jesus felt on Good Friday – and, more specifically, she could identify with those she had vowed to help.

Mother Teresa didn't come to her work with the poor from a position of power or status but one where the ground was a lot more level. Indeed, what status she had was broken by her 'dark night'. What she felt over those 50 years was the daily reality of so many of the poor, and so she spoke finally of being able to enter 'the dark holes' of the lives of those she had chosen to work with.

In those times when we feel abandoned, when we doubt, when we question those things we once thought to be certain – indeed in those times when we question the very efficacy of prayer – through Mother Teresa's example, we might come to realise it is perhaps there that we find the greatest encounter with our neighbours: words are abandoned, creeds put to the side and traditions stranded, and here we find that place where all we can do is listen to each other.

It is perhaps the most frightening description of prayer, but equally perhaps the deepest, most profound moment of encounter.

Written by RODDY HAMILTON

PRAYER NOTES

Acknowledgements

The 52 chapters of *Pray Now* 'Stories of Encounter' were written by: Fyfe Blair, Derek Browning, James Cathcart, Adam Dillon, Roddy Hamilton, Ruth Harvey, Tina Kemp, Jo Love, David Lunan, Scott McKenna, Scott McRoberts, MaryAnn Rennie, Jock Stein, Lezley Stewart, Jenny Williams and Wendy Young.

Daily headline Scripture quotations are taken from the New Revised Standard Version, © 1989 Division of Christian Education of the National Council of Churches of Christ in the United States of America, published by Oxford University Press.

With special thanks to Phill Mellstrom, Felicity Burrows, Hugh Hillyard-Parker and Rosamund Connelly for their work in preparing the final manuscript.